ACCIDENTAL GRACE

• • • • • • • • • • • • • • •

POETRY, PRAYERS, AND PSALMS

Rami M. Shapiro

PARACLETE PRESS
BREWSTER, MASSACHUSETTS

2015 First Printing

Accidental Grace: Poetry, Prayers, and Psalms

Copyright © 2015 by Rami M. Shapiro

ISBN 978-1-61261-655-1

The Paraclete Press name and logo (dove on cross) is a trademark of Paraclete Press, Inc.

Library of Congress Cataloging-in-Publication Data
Shapiro, Rami M.
    Accidental grace : poetry, prayers, and psalms / Rami M. Shapiro.
    pages cm
    ISBN 978-1-61261-655-1
    1. Spiritual life. 2. Religious literature. 3. Prayers. 4. Religious poetry. I. Title.
    BL624.S4823 2015
    204'.32--dc23
                                    2015014127

10 9 8 7 6 5 4 3 2 1

Published by Paraclete Press
Brewster, Massachusetts
www.paracletepress.com
Printed in the United States of America

CONTENTS

INTRODUCTION

* * *

I became a poet in 1969. I was studying Jewish philosophy at the University of Tel Aviv—wait; that's not entirely true.

I was enrolled in the university's Department of Philosophy, but I spent as much time as I could among the mystics. I came to Israel as a student of Zen. I wanted to go home a student of Hasidism.

Hasidism was a Jewish revival movement founded in the 1700s by a charismatic rabbi named Israel ben Eliezer, whom the people called the Baal Shem Tov, the Good Master of the Name. The Name was the Name of God that mystics were using to heal people. Most of these healers—*Baalei Shem*, Masters of the Name—were con artists selling snake oil to the suffering Jews of Eastern Europe. Israel ben Eliezer was different. He had integrity. He was selling joy, and the cost was your addiction to despair. He was the Good Master of the Name. I wanted to be his disciple.

The problem was he died in 1760. I was 209 years too late. The Hasidim of my time were not to my liking. They were— as silly as it must sound when talking about people who are defined as ultrareligious—too religious. I wasn't interested in religion with all its rules and restrictions. I was interested in spiritual anarchy, a kind of free-for-all spiritual ecstasy I associated with Hasidism because I mistook the Hasidic fantasies of Martin Buber—who was himself a spiritual anarchist—for the Hasidism of my day. The Hasidim I met were much closer to the Orthodox Jews among whom I was raised than the wild, crazy wisdom teachers of the Baal Shem's inner circle.

And then came Rabbi Reuven.

RABBI REUVEN

Tall, rail-thin, in his early forties, and barely clinging to the mundane world, Reuven was, if you'll excuse my mixing cultural metaphors, a *ronin* among Hasidim; he was a leaderless samurai for God who was building a *kabbalah* study center in the Negev desert. He had the land. He had several buildings up and running. But he needed students: students to plow the soil of Torah on *Shabbos*, and students to till the soil of the Negev during the week.

Reuven was the rebbe I was looking for. Or so I thought. I would escape the campus confines with its focus on the historical-critical reading of Hasidic texts, and take refuge in the funky Hasidism of Reb Reuven. Reuven was not my first guru, but he was my first guru who demanded I dig trenches. He was the first guru who thought blisters on my palms were a sign of service to God. It didn't take this suburban Jew from western Massachusetts long to realize I wanted to study texts rather than pull stumps, and in time I stopped visiting the rebbe. But I was with him long enough to become a poet.

I BECOME A POET

Reuven was single, and while he seemed to follow the strict halakhic code of avoiding contact with women to whom he was not related by blood, he nonetheless allowed women to attend his classes. They could even work the fields. I mention this not to reveal some sexual scandal, but because I became a poet with a woman in the room.

I was standing with Reuven greeting students as they arrived for *Shabbos*. I had no idea why I had been given this task, but I was happy to do it. A very attractive young American woman came in and lit up a cigarette. Reuven, too, was a smoker, and he asked her for a cigarette. She popped one in her mouth, lit it, and then handed it to Reb Reuven. He declined. She looked to me for an explanation, assuming that must be the reason I was standing with the rebbe at the door. I explained that he could not take the cigarette from her hand let alone her lips due to the laws prohibiting men from coming into contact with women who were not their relatives.

She tossed the pack of cigarettes to me, and I handed one to the rebbe, who lit it and happily sucked in the last stream of nicotine before *Shabbos* made the lighting of fire, even one as small as a match, illegal. I returned the cigarette pack to the woman and wished her a good *Shabbos*. She returned the greeting, and turned to Reuven for further guidance, but he had already walked away to announce to the gathering community that we would have a reading from an American poet that evening after *Shabbos* dinner.

Excited, I asked him who this poet was. "You," he said. "You're the poet and you will give the reading." That's the moment I became a poet.

I had no idea what Reuven was talking about. I had published some poetry in the Tel Aviv University English-language student paper; that wasn't because the poetry was any good, but because I was the editor of the paper. And I was fairly certain Rabbi Reuven had never read that particular quarterly.

He was certain I was a poet, however, and just as certain that I had material with me that I could read aloud after *Shabbos* dinner. He was right: I did have poems with me, and I knew how to read. So I read them. That's the moment I became a poet who read his work aloud in public.

BACK HOME

By the time my blisters had broken and healed, I had lost touch with Rabbi Reuven. By the time I got home to Massachusetts, my love of Hasidism had faded away as well. I went back to Zen Buddhist studies, enrolling full time (due to special dispensation) in the Department of Religion at Smith College under the guidance of Rev. Dr. Tetsuo Unno and his Zen master Joshu Sasaki Roshi of Mount Baldy.

I intended to become a Zen Buddhist, both academically and practically. My first Zen meditation intensive with Sasaki Roshi, called a *sesshin* (the word is Japanese for "touching the heart-mind"), was run by his *jikijitsu*, his directing monk. The *jikijitsu* was Leonard Cohen. Yeah, *that* Leonard Cohen. Of course, we didn't call him Leonard. He had a Zen Buddhist name, "Jikan" (Silent One), and that is what we called him.

We were instructed not to talk with Jikan about his work as Leonard Cohen, and we held strictly to that demand. I had enough distractions keeping me from enlightenment and had no use for worshiping this Canadian Jewish poet and folksinger. But I did talk with him, and as I did it dawned on me that Zen welcomed poets and Jews, and since I was officially both I felt all the more confident that I would find a place in the Zen world.

Two years later Sasaki Roshi called my bluff. At the end of yet another *sesshin* he challenged me to skip graduate school and move to Mount Baldy and become, like Jikan, a real Zen monk. If someone else had asked me about this, I would have paused, smiled just enough to let the questioner know that if I wanted to become a real Zen monk, I could, and then said, "I'm thinking about doing just that." But this wasn't "someone else"; this was Roshi. Here was my new koan: to be or not to be a Zen monk, that is the question.

"Oh, Roshi," I blurted out without a moment's thought, "I can't do that. I'm going to be a rabbi!"

"Good," Roshi said in his heavily accented Japanese rumble. "Be a rabbi. Be a Zen rabbi!" That was the last time Roshi and I spoke privately. But I did as he said, and became a Zen rabbi.

A ZEN RABBI

At first I thought a Zen rabbi was a rabbi who wrapped a *tallit*/prayer shawl around the Buddha: making Buddhism kosher by finding ways to read Buddhism into Jewish text and tradition. I wasn't wrong, but I wasn't quite right.

As it turns out, a Zen rabbi is a rabbi who isn't all that concerned with being a rabbi or a Jew. A Zen rabbi is a rabbi who, if she met Buddha on the road, wouldn't kill him, but would take him out for bagels and lox. A Zen rabbi is a rabbi who thinks that God is reality manifesting as everything, the way an ocean manifests as waves. A Zen rabbi is a rabbi who doesn't see tradition as an end, but a means to an end. And the end isn't enlightenment but the end of enlightenment.

A Zen rabbi is also a poet.

I became a Zen rabbi in 1981. I was given *smicha*, a certificate of ordination, and a check for $500, my half of the Bettan Memorial Prize for Creativity in the Liturgical Arts, which I had won for my poetry. The other half went to my friend Beat Rabbi James Stone Goodman, whom I have never ceased to love, and never ceased to envy for having the primo-cool middle name "Stone." If I had his name, I would cut off the "James" and the "Goodman" and just be "Stone." But my middle name is "Mark," so I cut that off along with my last name and became just Rami. Rabbi Rami. Zen rabbi Rami. A poet.

As it turns out, no synagogue was looking to hire either Zen rabbis or poets that year, and I had to create my own, which I did. I stayed there twenty years and then knew I had to move. No reason; I just knew. So I did.

Most of my poetry comes from those twenty years of being a Zen rabbi: wrestling with Jewish texts, teachings, and traditions and feeding them through the Zen shredder of my evermore postreligion mind.

POET

Everything you will read in this collection has a hook in traditional Jewish texts. That doesn't mean these poems are Jewish; they aren't. I'm not even certain they're poems. All I know is that they arose out of the rubble of my endless shattering of traditional Jewish literature. These are not careful constructs, but messy reconstructions of even messier deconstructions.

My son, Aaron, is a poet. He writes about life. I'm a Zen rabbi who writes about nothing. My son writes cool; I write angry. I read traditional texts and become furious over how close they come to the truth without ever actually articulating it. And the angrier I get, the more violently I shred the material I'm supposed to love. I shred it into a heap and then toss the bits into the air and grab at those I can grasp and tie them into sentences and spit them out in ink on paper.

ACCIDENTAL GRACE

Life is accidental grace. I didn't ask to be here. I didn't plan to be here. I don't believe in past lives, and have a hard time even believing in this one. But I do know a few things, and the things I know I write down. And the things I write down often make it into books, and the books somehow make it into bookstores, and I often walk into those bookstores looking for those books to remind myself of what I knew, because I seem to know less and less.

But I keep writing.

This book was, like all my others, an accident of grace. Jon Sweeney of Paraclete Press e-mailed to see if I was interested in collecting my poetry. He knew me from his days at Jewish Lights and had published several of my books at both Jewish Lights and Paraclete.

But did I have poems that he could publish?

Rabbi Reuven thought I was a poet and had me read to my peers. Hebrew Union College thought I was a poet and gave me an award for it. Many editors of synagogue and church liturgies thought I was a poet, and have published my poems in prayer books, both Jewish and Christian.

But am I a poet?

I am still not entirely sure. I will leave that for you to decide.

PSALMS

PSALM 1

Do you want to be happy?

Ignore the counsel of the selfish;
avoid the path of the cruel;
refuse the company of nihilists.

Do you want to be happy?

Delight in life unfolding;
immerse yourself in what is as it is, from morning to night.

The wise are deep-rooted trees fed by streams of compassion,
their fruits ripening in tune with need and necessity,
and given freely to those in need.

The foolish are rootless chaff
blown aimlessly by ever-shifting desire,
and forever on the brink of exhaustion.
They cannot survive honest investigation,
nor can they profit among the kind and the just.

Compassion and justice guide the wise traveler,
while the foolish stumble over their own conceit,
offering shallow advice,
serving only themselves,
and empty of all joy.

PSALM 16

Lift from me this mask of separation;
awaken me to Life's grand pattern;
protect me as I seek Your refuge—
I so fear the letting go that is our embracing.
No words can depict You,
all words drive me from You.
No thoughts, no theories—idols all!
Only when my mind is clear,
can my heart be filled with the Wonder of You.
I would know You if I could but stand still;
but I wobble and doubt and cannot believe
that I can be that which I already am.
At night I am instructed:
in drifting thought and twisted dream
the Way is shown.
You are beside me always, I shall not stumble,
for even a fall is a journey and
no journey is in vain if
I would but take it up wholeheartedly.
Help my heart be joyous,
my soul exult.
I dwell secure in You.

PSALM 23

You alone shepherd me,
lessening my needs and fulfilling them.

Lying delighted in lush green pastures,
I know You are all.

Walking beside softly flowing waters,
following the watercourse way,
I seek the simple and embrace the subtle,
restoring my soul as an extension of You.

Even as I walk through life's valley shadowed by death,
I fear no separation for You are with me.

Like a shepherd's rod, You warn me of danger.
Like a shepherd's staff, You alert me to dis-ease.

You set a table of feasting between me and my enemies,
Inviting us to meet, and eat, and befriend the other within
    and without.

You cool my anger, and calm my fears.
Like water breaking a river's banks,
Your blessings overflow,
embracing the high but seeking the low.

When I walk with You and know it is You who walks as me,
I leave only goodness and mercy in my wake,
knowing every place is Your place, and every face is Your face.

Blessed are You who leads me to
walk with fierce and freeing faith
the pathless land to which You summon me.

PSALM 29

You are beyond imagining.
Your Name is Nameless.
You who are All cannot be any.
You who are nothing
speak through all things.
Oceans rumble, thunder rattles,
great cedars fall with a crash—
this is Your voice
and this too Your greater silence.
Nations crumble beneath the weight of their own arrogance.
People despair from their own greed.
This is the voice of Your justice:
no evil is prevented and no consequence softened.
We reap what we sow.

In the Temple all say "Glory!"
In the streets all cry "Chaos!"
Who can see the order in the whirlwind?
Who can see the pattern in the wildness?
Who dares cry "glory" in the midst of chaos?

Still the heart and attend to Chaos;
Still the mind and the Glory is heard.
Still the soul and whisper Amen.
In this there is salvation.
In this and this alone.

PSALM 32

Happy are they whose sins are forgiven,
who break the bonds of habitual evil.
Happy are they who harness evil
and turn it toward good,
who deceive neither self nor other,
but welcome both with mercy and compassion.

I know I have sinned,
but I fear to speak—
will not my admission mock me,
will I not become my own Adversary?
Yet my silence is a burden, my guilt chokes me,
my very being weighs heavy
and I no longer smile.

I groan with the weight of it,
but I fear to speak—not even to You,
especially not to You.

Day and night I struggle to be
who I imagine I am supposed to be
without really knowing who in fact I am.
I fear that I know,
or I know that I fear,
that I am wicked and selfish and far
from the One that pretends to be other.

The effort drains me,
I am forever tired and depressed.
The lie shrivels me,
I am a leaf without branch,
dry and shivering in the wind.
O let me admit my failings,
accept my guilt.

Let me silence the Lie
and confess the Truth:
I am neither bad nor good,
neither sinner nor saint—
but a blend of both:
a person conflicted and confused.
Let me confess and accept
and I will find the strength to repair what I have damaged;
the skill to mend what I have torn;
the compassion to heal what has been hurt.

Let all who seek the Way learn this:
that when misfortunes befall you, accept them;
if they come as a mighty wave, bend to them;
if you let them come, they will let you go;
if you seek to repel them, they will drown in a pool of despair.

You are my shelter, my Self.
You preserve me from distress
and surround me with joy—
but only if I admit and accept
who I am
and what I do.

PSALM 41

Though I know You are to me
as an ocean is to a wave,
I nevertheless feel
far from You,
other than you.

I am haunted by devils
puffing me up with perfumed breath,
flattering me with shallow talk,
distracting me from You
by insisting You are far from me.

I turn to trusted friends for guidance;
to beloved friends with whom I have shared my table and
    even my bed,
yet I reject their advice and
fail to break the spell of self–delusion.

And so I turn to You—

Lift me up even as I press myself down.
Let me reclaim my faith in friendship,
and heed the words of those who love me.

Let my fears give way to wonder, and
my illusions scatter like dry leaves.
Let my ignorance surrender to wisdom, and
my delusions fade like shadows at high noon.

In this way let me reclaim the truth and
find myself no longer apart from
but rather a part of
You who are all.

PSALM 42

As a thirsty deer
races toward fresh and flowing streams,
so am I racing toward You.

I am dry and brittle,
lost to living waters, and
surviving only on tears.

No one asks of the deer:
"Where is your stream?"
Yet everyone asks of me:
"Where is your God?"

The deer need not answer.
I cannot answer.

I remember being carried with the mob
to sing praises in Your House,
but I cannot recall the route for myself.
I remember giving thanks for gifts unending,
but I cannot recall receiving even one.

I am confronted with Your bounty and yet
I am myself barren. And yet . . .

Deep calls to deep within me;

Self calls to the self that is me;

Your thundering Voice pierces the distracting chatter;

I feel Your presence faintly, but distinctly. And I know:

I cannot find You because I cannot lose You.

I cannot see You because You are the seer.

I cannot know You because You are the knower.

I cannot race toward You because You are already here.

There is nothing I can do

for all doing is You.

All there is for me is surrender,

and even this You have done.

PSALM 59

Stalked by my own lusts,

threatened by my own desires and selfish passions,

I call to You:

Rescue me!

My calls are drowned out by the mocking within me:

"How pious your pleas! Does your god not know the shal-
    lowness of your love?"

It's true:

I am shallow, while You are deep.

I am effervescent foam on the surface of Your ocean.

Yet I beg to be swallowed into the depths of Your love.

Stir Yourself within me.

Awaken me to the truth that silences my lies.

Leave not even an echo of deceit within me.

PSALM 77

Your Way is just, balanced, and blending;

suffering is Your Way, and Love.

It cannot be other than It Is

other than You Are

other than I Am.

Suffering and Joy—twins!

Terror and Tears—twins!

Pain and Mercy—twins!

You and I—

Your Way is Wonder beyond words.

Your Presence fills all and is known by none.

The oceans behold You and tremble.
The clouds see You and spill forth their rain.
Your thunder deafens. Your lightning blinds.
Nothing can point and say: There is God!
For where are You not?

Your Way is no way.
Your Path is no path.

Your Way, all ways.
Your Path, all paths.
Your Place, all place,
my place, this place.

PSALM 90

Oh Holy One of Being,
You who are the Ground of all ground,
the Place of every place,
in You alone I seek refuge.

You are my Creator
drawing me up from of the earth as a beginning.
You are my Destroyer
pulling me back to her as an ending.

Birthing and dying are to You
what exhaling and inhaling are to me:
the flow and ebb of nature naturing.

Where I see lines, You see spirals.
Where my sight is bounded by horizons,
Yours sees the infinite enfolded in the finite.

To me my life is once upon a time;
to You it is once upon the timeless.

My birth is the echo of another's death;
My death is the echo of another's birth.
And all of this is You.

I imagine I know You,
and explain Your ways by referencing my fantasies.
But Your ways are not other than Your nature,
And you do what You do because You are what You are.

If I live seventy years or even eighty,
I will fail to know You as You are,
continuing to mistake the imaginings of my mind
for the truth of Your being.

Remove this ignorance from me, God,
that I might awaken to You, in You, as You.

PSALM 93

The earth is secure;
it is I who imagine her frailty.
The earth stands firm;
it is I who plot her downfall.
She is greater than me,
and includes me in a larger scheme.
I am her child
though not her only child.
I am her hope
though not her only hope.
I am one she grew
to see her own face,
to know her own mind,
to foster surprise.
I am one who can know I am One.

PSALM 95

Life is all from You and in You:
the valleys, the mountains
the shore and the sea.
And so am I—
This fragile reed

with beating heart and jumping mind;
this thinking bellows
breathed and breathing,
all You.
From You comes each
and to You each returns.
And in between is You as well.
You in anger and You in song,
You in play and You in pain,
You in danger and You in salvation,
it is all You and You are all there is.
I sing the wonders of all You are
and the simple truth of You is known.

PSALM 96

Sing to Life a new song!
Sing to Life, all Creation!
Sing of compassion and
Temper your deeds with kindness.
Sing to all the world and
Tell of the miracles that sustain us daily.
Yet wonder is greater than praise,
No words can capture its essence.
All words are idols, all ideas snares—

Truth is beyond opinion,

Reality lies beyond thought's last horizon.

Splendor and majesty leave us speechless,

Strength and beauty are touched not talked.

Let your worship be acts of beauty and holiness;

Let all the world stand together in awe.

Declare among the nations, "All is God! Maintain the world
with justice!"

The heavens rejoice and the earth is glad;

The seas roar their praise.

The fields exult; the forests sing.

For all the world is rooted in righteousness.

PSALM 97

Embedded in my heart is a melody.

I hear it now and again, faintly.

It disturbs my quest for power with hints of grace.

It haunts my dreams of control with intimations of selflessness.

It stays my hand lifted in anger

And softens my chest tight with rage.

It whispers to me of justice,

And sings to me of compassion.

It is the song of God and I shall sing it yet.

But not alone.

We each bear the song

And someday we will sing it together in harmony.

On that day mountains of discord will melt before us;

Idols of ego, tribe, and boundary will shatter,

And together we will sing the world awake.

PSALM 98

Sing to God a new song,

A song whose words not yet written

Speak a joy not yet felt;

Whose melody not yet composed

Evokes a harmony not yet imagined.

Sing to God a new song

With a new voice.

With lyre and with drum,

With voice and with silence,

Sing a song that surprises even God.

And in that surprise will be a great deliverance.

PSALM 99

The earth trembles with intimations of You.
The nations quake before the One without a flag.
Our boundaries shatter as the Whole hugs its parts.
We scar the earth with barbed lines
and define ourselves within them.
We label the stranger and mark a friend;
You are greater than this.
You are above our masks and our magic.
You speak and there are no words.
You teach and there are no books.
You guide and there are no gurus.
You plant justice and we sow discord.
You seed compassion and we reap anger.
You extend charity and we shrug indifference.
No wonder there is trembling.
We are frightened not of You but of ourselves.
We are frightened not of the One
but of the many we call "them."

May I make this moment a moment
of emptying myself of my self;
of exalting the One
who is at the heart of the many;
of humbling myself
before You who are all.

And in this way will I move beyond fragmentation
to the greater unity
that is Your gift and my essence.

PSALM 105

Open my heart with thanksgiving!
Open my lips with singing!
Open my eyes with the miracles
unfolding around and within me!

Let all I do be for Your sake.

I take comfort in the Ineffable for I am of It.
I take comfort in the Nameless
and rejoicing that I, too, have No Name.

Search for God;
beneath the surface there is holiness.
Seek out the Face;
it is reflected in all and all in It.

Remember past miracles,
awake to present wonders.
Remember the Unnamed and Unnameable;
the Silent, the Hidden, the Noisy and Revealed—
This is my God:
Life now!
Life here!

PSALM 137

By the rivers of Babylon
I collapse in tears
bemoaning my fate.

There was a time I believed in my own power.
I thought I could conjure You
through rite and ritual,
control You through psalm and sacrifice,
and make of You a fortress and shield against my enemies.

I was wrong,
and my error has cost me everything.
So I sit and weep
hoping my tears can do what my magic could not:
show me the truth.

If I forget you, O Jerusalem,
and again lift my sword in service to arrogance,
let my right hand shrivel.

If I abandon truth,
and again allow injustice to masquerade as deserved glory,
let my tongue stick to my mouth
reducing my speech to mumbling.

Ignorance has brought me here.
Arrogance is the cause of my ruin.

Let me remember how these
led to the crumbling of my city,
and the shattering of my Temple.

And let me give thanks to You for leading me here.

Please, God, silence the vengefulness within me
that justifies battering the babies of my enemies
on the rocks of their city until their bodies dissolve in pools
    of blood and fat.

Help me step beyond anger to humility,
beyond cruelty to kindness,
beyond hatred to forgiveness and love,
and in this way realize a new way of being as I sit by the
    waters of Babylon.

PSALM 139

You see me and know me.
You see my rising and my sitting,
my walking and my lying down.
You know my thoughts before I think them
and my words before I speak them.

You surround me front and back.
You envelop me above and below.
You permeate me the way wetness permeates a wave.

There is no I and You, only I in You,
only You in me, with me, as me.

The highest heaven is You;
the deepest hell no less so.
Dawn is You,
and dusk as well.
Light is You, and
shadow is You, and
there is nothing that You are not.

You knew me before there was a me to know.
You knit me together from the strands of life
and knotted me in ways that allowed me to know myself.

How can I fathom this?
How can this finite I know You, the Infinite I Am?
How can I the created know the Source of creativity?

You have given me everything,
yet I would ask for one thing more:

Make me as transparent to myself as I am to You
that at last I see as You see me,
and thus see You alone.

PSALM 150

Praise Life!
Praise Wonder!
look and see
listen and hear
taste and touch and smell
the awesome simplicity of This.

Praise Life!
in sacred places.
Praise Life!
through just acts and compassionate deeds.
Praise Life!
with upbeat horn, lilting harp, entrancing lyre.

Praise Life!
with drum and dance
violin and flute
clashing cymbals.

Let all that breathe
breathe praises!
Breathe in psalms
breathe out hymns.
Breathe and sing
and let joy resound
within you
and without you.

POEMS

I AM THE WORLD

I am the world.
Not separate or apart,
not one among many,
but many within One.

I am the world
birthing and dying,
growing young
and growing old.

I am the world
capable of sustaining
all in need
if I would but
give my self away.

KINDLING LIFE'S LIGHT

Darkness blankets me.
Comforting, perhaps a bit frightening.
It harbors both dreams and demons.
I tap it for solace. I delve it for options.
I flee it for fear that it mirrors that

which I wish so desperately to avoid: Me.
Yet I am here not to embrace the dark
but to kindle the light.
Not to close my eyes forever,
but to open them this once.
I dwell amid the dark and bring forth light.
Soft, fragile, flickering light.
The only light I know. The only light I can bear.
I bring it, yet it isn't mine.
I kindle it, yet it isn't me.
I am the light bearer only.

Where the world is dark with illness
let me kindle the light of healing.
Where the world is bleak with suffering,
let me kindle the light of caring.
Where the world is dimmed by lies
let me kindle the light of truth.

Blessed is the One beyond light and dark
Who yet is light and dark and
by whose power I sanctify all Life
with the light of my one life.

LIGHTING THE LIGHTS OF SABBATH

Two candles.
How small they seem,
these stark white reminders of ancient days;
how insignificant.
And yet they speak to me:
A waxed mime recounting lost dreams, old worlds, older
    visions.
I am drawn to them through habit and guilt,
fearful that if I do not light I will not be lighted
and an eternal darkness will swallow me
now and forever. . . .
And something Else.
Something I sense but cannot say;
something I taste but cannot swallow;
something Else.
I feel it in the match
and the fingers that tremble before the flame.
I feel it in the first charring of the wick
as it is martyred to the light.
I feel it in the first melting of the wax
as paraffin tears tumble
then freeze
on bone white cheeks.
Bubbe is here. And Zayde.

The old and the eternally aging.
And something Else.
I light because I must.
By this light I am led,
with this lighting I lead.

THERE IS A HUNGER

There is a hunger in me no thing can fill;
a gnawing emptiness that calls forth dreams
dark and unfathomable.
My soul is whispering; Deep calling Deep,
and I know not how to respond.
The Beloved is near—as near as my breath,
as close as my breathing—
The World Soul of which my soul
is but a sliver of light.
Let me run to it in love,
embracing the One who is me,
that I might embrace others who are One.
Enwrapped in Your Being
I am at peace with my becoming.
Engulfed in Your flame
I am clear and unclouded.
I am a window for the Light,

a lens by which You see Yourself;
a slight of Mind
that lets me know me as You
and lets You know You as me.
How wondrous this One
Who is the Face of all things.

WELCOMING ANGELS

In the arduous simplicity of this moment
I open my heart, mind, and soul to stillness.
In the deeper quiet
I sense the greater Life that is my life.
I do not live only; I am lived.
I do not breathe only; I am breathed.
I am not only the one I appear to be
but also the One who appears as me.

In the arduous simplicity of this moment
I open my heart to compassion,
my mind to wisdom,
my soul to the round of birth, death, and rebirth.

From this openness I welcome messengers of God,
angels who embrace me with blessing.
If I am compassionate and just they bless me:
"So may you be tomorrow as well."
If I am mean and selfish they bless me:
"So may you be tomorrow as well."
The blessing is theirs. The reality always mine.
Welcome, my friends, to my soul's quiet.

SPIRIT'S WAY

The way of the spirit is the way of the feminine,
the receptive,
the creative,
the birthing,
the way that takes in
in order to transform and
then to return
to what is
something that never was.

She rests within me.

I smile softly and open to her.

I breathe easily and welcome her.

I close my eyes to all becoming

and revel for a moment in the magic of just being.

I feel her kiss upon my brow.

Don't be ashamed, she whispers, we have all fallen.

Don't be distressed, we have all erred.

There is none who is not soiled.

We are simple in foolishness, and simpler still in wisdom.

For the greater truth is the ultimate simplicity.

Yes! I welcome the Bride!

Let Her shine through my eyes. Let Her laugh through
my mouth.

Let Her dance through my feet. Let Her hold through my
arms.

Welcome sweet Bride.

Come in peace. Come in, Peace.

ATTENDING

Here I am—waiting.
Watching.
Listening.
Attending to what is within and without.
Your whispered breath fills me with wonder and wisdom,
and I bend embraced by You who are all.
For a moment I no longer breathe,
I am breathed.
For an instant I know the truth of who I am—Your breath,
a fleeting exhalation of
All into This.
How wondrous this moment
when breath breathes and knows itself Divine!

WONDER

Each night I marvel: the fading light!
The deepening darkness!
Each morning I exclaim:
The dawn gates open wisely,
understanding marks the day's divisions.
Season follows season,
and the sky is patterned with orbiting stars.

Order amid the greater chaos,
and the greater chaos amid
an even Greater Order—
this world rests on the shores of wonder.
What mind orders the wildness, fashions the void?
You, my Source and my Substance,
You create day and night.
You roll away light before dark
and dark before light.
In You is the shadowplay of
all being and becoming.
And in You I rest and struggle,
seeking to do as You do:
order the chaos
and set wisdom and understanding firm.

I AM LOVED

I am loved.
Too easy to say, perhaps.
Too fleeting a feeling upon which to anchor a life.
And yet it is so.
I am loved. Though not always by me.
From my earliest days I was helped and guided
to find the path of justice, mercy, and humility.

Some guides were clear:
parents, grandparents, teachers, friends.
Some were subtle, rarely expected,
often painful.
They are all and always with me.
When I quiet my mind and still my heart;
when I cease the nervous doing
that so often passes for purposeful living;
I sense their wisdom still
murmuring in my heart.
I call out and hear the echo;
my voice no longer mine, and richer.
I listen and learn,
and plant my feet on the path of righteousness.

UNENDING LOVE

I am loved by an unending love.
I am embraced by arms that find me
even when I am hidden from myself.
I am touched by fingers that soothe me
even when I am too proud for soothing.
I am counseled by voices that guide me
even when I am too embittered to hear.
I am loved by an unending love.

I am supported by hands that uplift me
even in the midst of a fall.
I am urged on by eyes that meet me
even when I am too weak for meeting.
I am loved by an unending love.

Embraced, touched, soothed, and counseled;
may mine too be the arms and the fingers,
the voice and the hands,
the eyes and the smile
that compels another to say:
"I am loved by an unending love."

MORE DARKNESS THAN LIGHT

There is more darkness than light.
Yet light enough to see this place
where I stand and
where I might next step.
Light enough
to step one step
to turn one turn
at a time this time
Now.

Yes there is pain and suffering.
And there is redemption.
With the pain,
With the suffering,
There is redemption.

Who can straighten the crooked?
I can't, but wish it otherwise.
Otherwise has trapped me too long.

Now is the time of arising.
Now is the time of awakening.
Now is the time of doing;
not straightening
but no more twisting;
not forgetting
but at last forgiving.
And to that I say: Amen.

UNITY

Listen! Listen!
Still the mind's chatter,
quiet the heart's desire.
The rush of life flows through me.
The heart of eternity beats in my own chest. Listen.
I am the fingers of a divine and infinite hand.
I am the thoughts of a divine and infinite mind.
There is only One Reality,
the Singular Source and Substance of all diversity.
This One alone is You.
You alone are me.

AND YOU SHALL LOVE

Having heard the One, I know myself commanded:
With all my heart: love Life—
feel freely, feel fully, act wisely.
With all my mind: love Life—
let no opinion make truth taboo.
With all my strength: love Life—
be in the world with purpose and presence.

Set Truth upon your heart and let not
the One become lost in the many.
Glove your hands with compassion
that your deeds be just.
Open your eyes to wisdom
that your vision be daring and true.
Set these words
upon the doorposts of your house
and upon your gates
that your going out and your coming in
be for peace.
(after Deuteronomy 6:4–9)

RESPONSIBILITY

If I follow the way I have been shown,
the way of justice, mercy, and humility,
serving Life with the fullness of my life,
the earth will flourish
with righteousness and riches.
Pure rain will fall in its season, for I will scrub clean the sky;
earth will bring forth her bounty, for I will heal her wounds;
the fragrance of life will scent the air like fine oil,
for the stench of my pride will fade as I embrace humility.
There will be food enough for all,
and all will be able to partake of it.

No one will exploit another,
for no other shall be separate from the One.

But beware! If I follow another path,
pursuing gods of narrow desire
who separate one from another
in quest of power and control,
then the heavens will rain poison,
Creation will fall ill, and I and all
will soon disappear from this good earth.

Therefore, I impress these words upon my heart to quell anger;
I bind them on my hands to stop violence;
I set them before my eyes to see the One who is all as all.
Then my days and the days of my kind will endure, with
generations passing righteousness and kindness one to the
    other
all the days of the earth.
(after Deuteronomy 11:13–21)

TRUTH

I affirm this simple truth:
You are the Source and Substance of All.
Creation is the Infinite manifest as the finite;
there is only You,
empty of form, taking all form.

Knowing this I let go the compulsion to rule,
the desire to control others.
Rooted in this I learn to judge well,
uprooting oppression within and without.
You create wonders surpassing my understanding,
marvelous things beyond reckoning.
No science can fully know,
no dogma can even pretend to map
that which is beyond thought.
Yet it is You that sustains me and all things.
In You there is no faltering,
my every step is guided by forces beyond my ken.
Nothing is by chance,
for even chance keeps its own order.
Let me mourn even my enemy's loss
taking no comfort in anyone's undoing.
For compassion is the way, even as is justice.

THIS IS MY GOD

Among all the gods I can name,
which compares to You, the One Beyond Naming?
Among all the quantities I can label,
number, mark, and measure,
which compares to You,

the Truth at the heart of Reality?
You are my God,
Nameless Source and Substance of all.
You and You alone exist.

LIVE EACH DAY

May I live each day with fullness of mind,
attending to Life and all she places before me.
Thus will I live without hesitation.
Only then can I lie down in peace,
having given Life my all.
Only then can I rise up
in anticipation of a new day,
knowing I have so much more to give.
Let compassion refine my actions,
and justice shield me from selfishness.
Let my life be a vehicle for grace and mercy,
bringing peace and comfort to all in need.
May the Source of Life spread a blanket of peace
over me,
over my community, and
over all the world.

RENEWAL

Life isn't only doing.
Stillness, too, is life.
And in that stillness
my mind cluttered with busyness quiets,
my heart racing to win rests,
and I hear Your whispered truths.

May the time soon come when I can
listen without speaking,
speak without scheming,
act without prejudice.

May I learn to enter the Silence
and there encounter the Ineffable.
May I learn to live without labels
and thus meet the Nameless.

Let me establish peace throughout the world,
letting justice and mercy shape all my deeds.

May the time soon come when I
and all the world sanctify Life with truth,
drawing upon the Source of Peace
to make peace in our own lives.

WHO IS GOD?

The Eternal God is not the
God of Abraham is not the
God of Isaac is not the God of Jacob is not the
God of Sarah is not the God of Rebecca is not the
God of Leah is not the God of Rachel is not the
God of my childhood is not the
God of my youth is not the
God of my adulthood is not the
God of my old age is not the
God of my dying is not the God of my imagining.
The Eternal God is not my creation.

The Eternal God is not the
God who chooses is not the
God who commands is not the
God who punishes is not the
God who creates is not the
God who destroys is not the
God who makes me win is not the
God who sees that my enemies lose.
The Eternal God is not my creation.

The Eternal God is the
God who alone exists and who exists alone.
When I am free from ancestors, free from traditions,
free from truths, free from words, free from thoughts,

free from even the need to be free,
there is God and there I am not.

YOU ALONE

You are it:
Birth and death,
joy and sadness,
success and failure,
courage and fear—it's all You.

All things and their complements come from You.
All things and their complements are You.

May I open my eyes to see You as You
and not as I so desperately want You to be.
May I see that time and eternity
are but shadows of now,
and that true immortality
is to die to time and
awake to the deathless present that is You.

REST

You capped doing with nondoing;
You blessed becoming with being;
You honored labor and rest.
Rest reveals the importance of work.
Work reveals the importance of rest.
The two together make the world;
the two together make a human being.
I rest when I cease my struggle to control.
I rest when I abandon my pride of ownership.
I rest when I give thanks for what is.

SET ASIDE THESE MOMENTS

I set aside these moments
to revel in Your work by sharing Your rest.
I set aside these moments
for mindfulness and renewal.
I set aside these moments
to review my mission and my priorities.
I set aside these moments
to honor all that I have been given.
I set aside these moments
to take stock of all that I am.

WHY PRAY?

For what do I pray?
For health?
For happiness?
For wealth or fame?
Who can say what will befall me?
I do what I do in pursuit of what I desire,
but the hunt only is mine; the capture is in other hands.
I pray for nothing, for I am nothing.
My desires are not Yours.
My needs are not Yours,
perhaps not even mine.
I pray simply to be in Your presence.
I pray simply to be and be present.
For that is all I can do: be and be present.
Present to You and what You bring this moment
and this moment again.
All there is is You;
Time and eternity, self and other—all You.
So I pray to pray.
I pray to be aware of the Being that is all becoming
And the Becoming that is all being.
All and nothing,
here and there,
now and forever,
You alone.

SPIRITUALITY

Spirituality is living with attention.
Living with attention leads me to thanksgiving.
Thanksgiving is my response
to the great debt I accrue with each breath.
Attending to the everyday miracles of ordinary living
I am aware of the interconnectedness of all things.
I cannot be without You.
This cannot be without That.
Each cannot be without All.
And All cannot be without every.
Thanksgiving is not for anything,
it is from everything.
May I cultivate the attention
to allow the thanks that is Life
to shape the dance that is my living.

PEACE

Peace is not the absence of conflict.
Peace is dealing with conflict
while honoring justice.
Peace is not the absence of anger.
Peace is expressing anger

while honoring compassion.

Peace is not the absence of desire.

Peace is allowing for desire without

the fantasy that fulfillment brings happiness.

Peace is not the absence of fear.

Peace is knowing how to move through fear.

Peace is not the absence of self.

Peace is knowing that the self is absent.

May I cultivate the skills to live in peace:

to live with honor,

to live with justice,

to live with compassion,

to live with desire,

to live with fear,

to live with self,

to live with emptiness.

SPEECH

Let me attend to my words,

taking care to say what I mean and do what I say.

Let me guard my tongue from evil

and my lips from speaking falsehood.

Let me rise above those who slander me,

and take care not to slander others.

Let me forgive those who offend against me,
and take care to offend only the unjust.
Let me open my heart to Reality
and find in Her Wisdom my way to righteousness.

GOD IS HOLINESS

God is holiness emptying into creation.
God is creation emptying into consciousness.
God is consciousness emptying into self.
God is self emptying into Self.
God is Self emptying into holiness.
God is holiness . . .

ATTENTION

I stand at attention
not rigid or fixed, but relaxed and alert.
Addressed by Life,
commanded by history and circumstance,
I dare heed Your call:
do justly, love mercy, walk humbly with
You, Source and Substance of all.

I empty myself of distraction.

For a moment—peace.

The peace of being present,

the peace of being in place,

the peace of acting without hesitation,

the peace of attending without preoccupation.

I place my hope in You,

the One who is hope and promise,

the One who is deed and doer.

I place my hope in the wisdom of Your Way.

I cleanse my eyes of idols

and see Your presence in the world

as the world.

I empty my heart of tyrants:

I am enslaved to nothing,

and no one is enslaved to me.

I recognize the limits of words and

go beyond labels to embrace each and every as One.

Then all who live will know

that to You alone I am loyal.

To You alone I am surrendered.

To You alone is the honor and the glory.

For You alone are Life

and all who are given to live it.

WHAT TO DO

Here is my charge:
Magnify and sanctify
Truth throughout the world.
Establish peace and harmony;
share the suffering;
reach out to those in need,
helping them lay down their burden
or shoulder it more powerfully.
There is a suffering that is natural to Life.
Yet so much of what I bear
is an unnecessary burden,
arising not from Life but from fear,
not from living with death but from dying to Life.

And here is my promise:
I shall learn to accept necessary suffering,
and put down unnecessary suffering
and let go the jagged hurts
that I have created for myself.

I shall allow my pain to give rise to compassion—
compassion for myself,
compassion for others.
I shall invoke the Power that makes for peace
throughout the heavens
and draw upon it

to make for peace
in my own life and
in the world in which I unfold.

LIFE

Birth and death,
a twisted vine sharing a single root.
A water bright green
stretching to top a twisted yellow
only to wither itself
as another green unfolds overhead.
One leaf atop another
and under the next.
A vibrant tapestry of arcs and falls
all in the act of becoming.
Death is the passing of life.
And Life—
the stringing together of so many little passings.

DISTINCTION

Darkness and light,
twins of a single mother birthing
all and nothingness with each breath.
We cannot know one while ignoring the other;
we cannot trust one while distrusting the other;
we cannot embrace one while fleeing the other;
we are the one, we are the other.

Light and dark, in and out, up and down—
each known only from the other.
Male and female, good and evil, right and wrong—
each incomprehensible without the other.

There are no singularities,
no lonely bits of drifting log afloat in a cosmic sea.
There is only Unity-in-Diversity,
only the on/off pulsating rhythms of life
beating first one then another of an infinite series of
gongs and clangs and drums and whispers
each singing the magic of creation.

There are no opposites, only polarities,
only the interrelatedness of things,
only the interdependence of the Many and the One.

Not one, not two;
Not different, not alike;
Not either, not or;
But and.

HIDDEN FACES

Whose is the Face behind the mask?
Is it mine?
So I thought
once;
but I'm not the Face but the mask.
Not the wearer but the worn,
not the player but the played.
I am a hollow reed
through which blows a soft wind.
Together reed and wind make music,
alone they are mute.
But let neither imagine itself to be the tune;
the magic arises not from the flute or the breath,
but from the meeting of the two.
The wonder is not in the mask or the Face,
but in the wearing and the meeting and the humor of it all.

ATTENTION

Attention is the ability to totally engage body, mind, and spirit
in the task at hand,
and thus see the infinite playing as the finite.

I pass through Life in a daze,
convinced that the ordinary events of every day
are (of all things!) profane
and not worthy of my undivided attention.
So I divide my attention—and therefore myself—
losing sight of the Unity implicit in Diversity.

Having devalued the ordinary
I seek refuge in the extra-ordinary,
becoming dependent upon those who encourage
my disparagement of the profane,
thus strengthening their monopoly of the sacred.

Attention is the re-membering of a forgotten Unity.

Attention demands
the abandonment of both sacred and profane.
It negates the monopoly of the priest,
and re-turns me to the awareness of Self
in every act of self.

For the person with attention,
every day
becomes the very day
upon which all Universe depends.

ANOTHER WORD

I wish there were another word for love,
a word as yet unspoken, not yet heard;
a word unformed,
uncut,
primal and raw.

With such a word I could sing to You
of feelings too swift for poet's tongue,
of pain too coarse for printer's page,
of softness too light for breathless sighs.

With such a word I could speak to You.

But I have no word,
no word but
love
and love will have to do
what no word in truth can ever do:
speak to me
of knowing You.

TO THE RIGHT, TO THE LEFT

To the right
to the left
   who shall live
   who shall die
To the right
to the left
   who by gassing
   who by labor
To the right
to the left
   who by fire
   who by fever
To the right
to the left
   who by suffocation
   who by beating
To the right
to the left
   who by Nazis
   who by kapos
To the right
to the left
   who shall live
   who shall die
and who shall survive to praise the difference?

MEMORY

Hard work,
this memory.
Reliving the past,
making it over
to my most current specifications
as if the
original first-time-aroundness of things
was not good enough.

Memory isn't recall,
it's remake.
A second chance;
to do what I should have done,
to say what I should have said,
to silence what I actually said.

Memory is a censor
replacing the original sensor.
It is a producer, an editor,
a critic with the audacity to rewrite the play in its own image.

In memory
I move from actor to reactor.
I excerpt, replay, rewrite
where once I could only go along.

This is the beauty of memory: it lies.
And if I need them badly enough
Memory's lies become my sacred truths.

A PRAYER FOR HONESTY

Dear One,
I open my mouth
to utter words of Truth.
May my speech
not compound the Simple.

FREEDOM

What is it I seek?
Freedom from? Freedom to?
No: freedom for!
May I cultivate the strength
to see what must be done
and to do it.

THE WAY WE WALK

Like a tree tangled
and strong,
the Way I walk
is right;
right,
but not straight.

IN THE QUIET OF MY SOUL

In the quiet of my soul
I feel the beating of You.

You are not other than I
nor am I other than You.
As wave is to ocean so am I to You.

Blessed are You, both Birther and Birthed!
How wondrous it is that I am born,
sustained, and brought
to this moment of turning.

THIS IS TORAH

Our sages said:
Whatever a faithful student will receive and transmit;
this is Torah.
However we find ourselves addressed
by the Shofar blast of Truth;
this is Torah.
Whenever we stand humbled by Eternity,
our hearts filled with love,
our arms outstretched
to lift up the fallen,
free the captive,
embrace the lost—
this, too, is Torah.

Sinai is ever present.
Wherever we gather to seek Wisdom;
However we struggle to renew the covenant,
to discover the Way;
Whenever we listen and hear,
receive, and transmit;
we stand at Sinai.

RECEIVE AND TRANSMIT

In each age
we receive and transmit Torah.
At each moment
we are addressed by the World.
In each age
we are challenged
by our ancient Teaching.
At each moment
we stand face to Face with Truth.
In each age
we add our wisdom
to that which has gone before.
At each moment
the knowing heart
is filled with wonder.
In each age
the children of Torah
become its builders
and seek to set the world firm on a foundation of Truth.

May we find in the Teachings of our prophets and sages,
our rebbes and storytellers,
our artists and wonder-workers,
a mitzvah for our time;

a law of life
that will repair the world
with peace.

WHISPERED WISDOM

Torah is a guide,
a voice, a whisper of Wisdom
echoing within and without.
Her mitzvot commit us to justice.
Her teachings move us to compassion.
Her stories bring us to attention
that we might be present to life's everyday wonders.
May the words of Torah be pleasant in our mouths.
May we and our children and our children's children
come to study Torah as a gateway to Truth and Love.
May we hearken to the voice of Sinai
addressing us now and here.
May we be moved to exclaim the mystery of Life
revealed in the rising sun,
the rustling tree,
the child's cry,
and a friend's embrace.
Blessed are those who bring Torah to the world.

A PARENT'S PRAYER

I thank You for this wondrous gift of life.
I am humbled by the blessings
and responsibilities of parenthood
and my participation in the miracle of creation.

May I learn to love without smothering.
May I learn to house without imprisoning.
May I learn to give without imposing.
May I learn to live today,
that yesterday and tomorrow
might find their own way in the world.

I give thanks to Life for the gift of life,
and stand in wonder
before the awesome task of parenting that lies before me.
Blessed is the Way of Life
that makes parent rejoice with child.

GOD IS

God is the Suchness
        of things as they are in and of themselves.
God is the Unity
        beyond the One and the Many.

God is the imageless Zero
>
> that sustains all numbering.

God is the Sameness

>
> that makes us one family.

God is the Difference

>
> that fashions our uniqueness and individuality.

God is the Power

>
> that makes for freedom,
>
> justice,
>
> creativity, and
>
> truth.

FOR HEALING

There are moments when wellness escapes me,
moments when pain and suffering
are not dim possibilities
but all too agonizing realities.
At such moments I must open myself to healing.

Much I can do for myself;
and what I can do
I must do.
But even when I do all I can do
there is, often,
still much left to be done.

And so I turn as well to healers
seeking their skill to aid in my struggle for wellness.
But even when they do all they can do
there is, often,
still much left to be done.
And so I turn to You,
to the vast Power of Being that animates the universe
as the ocean animates the wave.

And when I turn to You
I discover through pain and torment
the strength to live with grace and humor.
I discover through doubt and anguish
the strength to live with dignity and holiness.
I discover through suffering and fear
the strength to move forward into healing or unto death,
for both are You.

DEATH

There are no timely deaths,
though some are more accepted than others.
There are no blessed deaths,
though some are more peace-giving than others.
There are only unwanted deaths,
uncontrolled, unreasonable, unholy deaths.
Death tears at the marrow of the living,

shattering my facade of wisdom,

evoking the horror and the agony

of my own transience.

Yet even as I peer into the heart of death

and behold no answers,

a courage arises within me

to face the truth of my ignorance

with the light of my love.

Though I cannot know the reasons for death,

I can face the reality of it with the best of human dignity;

refusing to despair of life,

even as life seems to have despaired of me.

GATES

At each moment of our lives

we encounter gates behind which beckons the unknown.

We have little choice but to enter,

and, as we do,

the gates swing shut behind us.

We can never go back.

The known, the comfortable, the safe—

all these are in the past.

Only the unknown, the dangerous,

the mysterious, and the terrifying lay ahead.

Moving on makes us human,

doing so lightly and at peace makes us divine.

Eventually we come to the final gate,
the final closing.
The trail ends,
leaving behind only memories
of steps taken, leaps tried, grace achieved and shared.
How do we honor this final gate?
With tears and stories,
with memories and love,
with food and friends.
And with silence.

Silence is the heart of death,
and silence alone does it justice.
But silence does not mean passivity.
There are four virtues that form the core of silence.

The first is hearing:
hearing the inner voice of our pain and love,
rejoicing that nothing,
not even the grave,
can rob us of that supreme human emotion.

The second is memory:
reclaiming the past by refusing
to forget the joys it once held.

The third is action:

we must honor our dead by continuing to live ourselves.

Their memory is quickened only in the fullness of our own
   lives—

our own futures,

our own ongoing struggles

to make sense out of an often senseless world.

The fourth is wisdom:

every life is a teaching,

every person a guide to truth.

Hearing, memory, action, wisdom . . .

May each of these find a place in our silence, our grief,

and our moving out again into the world

where yet another gate beckons wide.

GRACE AFTER MEALS

My friends, let us give thanks for Wonder.

Let us give thanks for the Wonder of Life

that infuses all things now and forever.

Blessed is the Source of Life, the Fountain of Being,

the wellspring of goodness, compassion, and kindness

from which we draw to make for justice and peace.

From the creative power of Life we derive food and harvest,

from the bounty of the earth and the yield of the heavens
we are sustained and are able to sustain others.
All Life is holy, sacred,
worthy of respect and dignity.
Let us give thanks for the power of heart
to sense the holy in the midst of the simple.

We eat not simply to satisfy our own appetites,
we eat to sustain ourselves in the task we have been given.
Each of us is unique,
coming into the world with a gift no other can offer:
    ourselves.
We eat to nourish the vehicle of giving,
we eat to sustain our task of world repair,
our quest for harmony, peace, and justice.

We eat and we are revived, and we give thanks
to the lives that were ended to nourish our own.
May we merit their sacrifice, and honor their sparks of
    holiness
through our deeds of loving-kindness.

We give thanks to the Power that makes for Meeting,
for our table has been a place of dialogue and friendship.
We give thanks to Life.
May we never lose touch with the simple joy and wonder
of sharing a meal.

FRINGES OF BEING

Tallit wrapped,
held in angels' wings.
And if angels are too rare?
An autumn leaf soundlessly
suspended in air.
Be wrapped in that.

Tallit wrapped,
embraced in angels' wings,
we seek the One who supports the two,
the two that is at root One.
Our search is long and steep,
each step calling upon energy
the last was sure to exhaust.
And in the end?
Tallit wrapped,
embraced in angels' wings.

Tallit wrapped,
caressed by angels' wings,
we sit head bound to heart
and heart to hand
by black box and leather strand.
Tallit wrapped
we sit and breathe the breath of Adam.

DACHAU'S GOD

As we left Egypt's house of bondage
we worried:
Who is it that redeems Israel,
yet murders newborn babes?
>Can he not murder us as well?

As we crossed the parted Red Sea waters
we worried:
Who is it that redeems Israel,
yet drowns the people of Egypt?
>Can he not drown us as well?

As we lay, calf in hand, on Sinai's sands dying
we worried:
Who is it that redeems Israel,
yet slaughters those who mean only to serve him?
>Can he not slaughter us as well?

And as we shuffled heavily into the death of Dachau we
>chanted:
>Yes, yes, yes he can slaughter us as well.

Who is like you,
Dark and Brooding Lord?
Who so awesome and who so wild?
Who so tender and who so careless?
Who so faithful and who so wanton?

Who so loving that his passion fires blacken Europe's skies
    with our embrace?
        Who, My Lord, who?

OBLIGATED TO HOLINESS

Your Teaching obligates me to holiness:
"Be holy for I, God, am holy."
While I can never know You in the abstract
I am yet challenged to be You in the concrete.
How am I to practice Your Way of Holiness
and take up the norms of God?

Let me nurture benevolence:
opening the heart and giving comfort to those in need.
Let me cultivate compassion:
forgiving hurts, forgetting foolishness.
Let me be slow to anger and quick to do kindness.
Let me speak Truth and love mercy.
Let me do justly and root out evil.
Let me recognize my foolishness
and accept the mistakes of others with humor and grace.

And where better to begin
than here
and when better
than now?

WALK WISELY

The wise walk firmly,
knowing they do not know.
The foolish step gingerly
protecting their ignorance.
The wise walk lightly
bearing weightless truth.
The foolish step heavily
opinion scaring a path
in a purely pathless land.

TRUST IN GOD

Trust in God—

      trust the dark to scare you;

      trust the light to blind you;

      trust the dead to haunt you;

      trust the living to surprise you.

Trust in God—

      trust that love will last

      until it doesn't;

      trust that pain will endure

      until it passes.

Trust in God—

      love until you leave;
      live until you die.

Trust.

PORTIONS

Happy are they
for whom Life is divine.

Happy are they
whose home is in You, with You, as You.

Happy are they
whose portion is this:
the everyday wonders
of a divine and simple world.

FORGIVENESS

There is no forgiveness
save in reaching beyond;
there is no letting go
save in moving on.

Forgiveness is the courage to let go.

One doesn't pardon another;

one lets go of oneself,

thus allowing pain received and sustained,

hurt inflicted and imposed,

to settle,

and the true Self to rise.

WHAT WE FEAR MOST

What we fear most,

or so we say,

is that which is unknown.

But the unknown is just that—unknown

and therefore beyond fear.

What we fear in fact

is our projection of the known onto the unknown.

What we fear in fact

is our own shadow,

our own darkside painted large

across the canvas of the mind.

WHAT HURTS?

What hurts me tonight?
What troubles and haunts me?
What have I done
that I wish I had not done?
What have I felt
that I wish I had not felt?
What has happened to me that caused me pain?
What pain have I caused others?
I cannot undo what has been done.
I cannot unfeel what has been felt.
I cannot pretend to not hurting
unless I pretend to not caring.
But I do care.
And because I care, I hurt.
Living includes hurting,
and also healing.
Living includes mistakes,
and also correcting them.
It is not enough to be sorry;
it is only enough when I do rightly the next time.

WHAT NEXT?

When I understand that Life is moving on,
when I see that living is doing What Comes Next,
I discover that hurting is a part of life
but not all of life.
When I allow the hurting to happen
and then do what comes next,
I discover that just as there is hurt
there is also joy.
Sometimes I am happy
and sometimes I am sad,
but at all times I am confronted
by what comes next.
When happy—do what's next.
When sad—do what's next.

HEALING

Healing comes
when I take
my Place in the World
and re-pair the opposites
that so fragment my life.
Like pieces of a puzzle,

no two alike,
my coherence and well-being
are realized only
when I take my Place
and bring
my bit of uniqueness
to the Whole.

HALLOWING

It is up to us
to hallow Creation,
to respond to Life
with the fullness of our lives.
It is up to us
to meet the World,
to embrace the Whole
even as we wrestle
with its parts.
It is up to us
to repair the World
and to bind our lives to Truth.

So shake off the stiffness that keeps you
from the subtle
graces of Life
and the supple
gestures of Love.
With reverence
and thanksgiving
accept your destiny
and set for yourself
the task of redemption.

NEVER KNOWING

Despite all my prayers,
all my plans,
all my schemes,
I live in ignorance of tomorrow;
I exist in a state of perpetual never-knowing.

All I can be sure of
is that I can be sure of nothing at all.
Uncertainty is my only certainty;
I live in a fragile world of hopes and dreams and anxieties.

We live in a fragile world of constant change.

Don't ask, "Why?"

There is no why.

There is only the reality of change and not-knowing.

There is only the constant struggle

to make sense out of what so often appears senseless;

to make meaning out of what so often appears meaningless.

This is my task, our task:

to make meaning, to set purpose,

to discover the simple joys of living without illusion

in a world forever fragile and on the brink.

FRIENDS

To live is to suffer

and also to laugh;

to cry tears of anguish and also tears of joy.

Nothing is permanent:

neither pain nor gladness,

neither hurt nor happiness;

all is fleeting, all is fragile, all is empty of permanence.

Let me celebrate the holiness of impermanence.
Let me celebrate the awesomeness of change.
Let me give thanks
that even in the midst of this chaotic world
of fragile dwellings and broken hearts
I dare to reach out to another and whisper "friend."

HANUKKAH

The challenge and struggle of Hanukkah is all about us.
We find ourselves everywhere limited
by the boundaries of time and circumstance.
Uncertainty pervades existence,
and risk haunts everything we do.
Time and events flow beyond our control,
sweeping us swiftly on a surging tide.
The rush of things threatens to extinguish our light,
and often does,
leaving us,
if only for a single terrifying moment,
alone with our demons and the dark.

And yet the light returns.
From within or from without,
from an act of will or the strong arm of a friend,
from an inner vision or an oft-told tale,
from a heartfelt cry or a lover's kiss—
light returns.
We then take up the hammer of Judah
and boldly strike the anvil of gloom,
showering our world with sparks of light,
igniting flickers of hope,
nurturing the flames of new tomorrows.

This is Hanukkah's eternal message:
Darkness does not prevail; light returns.
Humankind, finite though it may be,
can yet affirm life's value.
Rejoicing in the will and the courage to be free,
we affirm life's meaning
and rededicate ourselves to its unfolding
through our Festival of Lights.
We do this as individuals and as families,
as separate selves and as community builders.
We do this as seekers and as sharers,
as teachers and as students.
We do this as an affirmation of the value of light,
with the recognition of the importance of darkness,
and the daring of a people risking all
in the heart of life's shadowplay.

SURRENDER

I call upon the Source of Life,
the Power within and without,
the Power that makes for
Being and Nothingness,
joy and pain,
suffering and delight.

I call upon You to calm my fearful soul,
to open me to the Wonder of Truth,
the transience of all things.

In Wonder was I conceived
and in Wonder have I found my being.
Thus I call upon You, the Source of Wonder,
to open my heart to healing.

In You I discover the mystery of Life
and the necessity of Death.
In You I see all things and their opposites
not as warring parties
but as partners in a dance
whose rhythm is none other
than the beating of my own soul.

Denial may come, but so too will acceptance.
Anger may come, but so too will calm.
I have bargained with my fears
and found them unwilling to compromise.
So now I turn to You,
to the Wonder that is my True Nature.

I abandon the false notions of separateness
and embrace the Unity that is my true Reality.
I surrender not to the inevitable but to Surprise,
for it is the impossible that is Life's most precious gift.
My tears will pass
and so will my laughter.
But I will not be silenced,
for I will sing the praises of Wonder
through sickness and health;
knowing that in the end,
this too shall pass.

UNVEILING

(In Jewish tradition it is customary to remove a veil covering on a new headstone at the first anniversary of a death.)

In the eyes of eternity,
a thousand years are but a day,
our lives but a fleeting hour.
We arise to life,
as a wave cresting upon a vast and shoreless sea.
And we abandon life
as a wave abandons its shape
and returns to the source from which it swelled.
Arising, dissolving, returning yet never leaving,
we are one with the eternal Source of Life now and forever.

The ragged tear death has rent in the fabric of our lives
cannot be mended.
Yet love is as strong as death;
and the bonds of love know no boundaries.
We still meet,
we still love;
if not in the world of physical reality
then in the gentler world of dream and memory.

The veil we remove
is but an outward sign
of an inner hiddenness.
When a loved one dies

there is often much fear
and anger and frustration and pain.
When a loved one dies we sometimes seek
to hide from the death
and veil ourselves from friends and memories.
But with this unveiling
we let go the hurt and fear,
we make peace with the living and the dead.
Out of respect for our loved,
out of respect for our grief,
out of respect for our continuing obligations
to self and others,
to life and to community,
we remove the veil
and embrace the love
that so desperately wishes to envelop us.

MEDITATION

Meditation means, quite literally,
to observe oneself.

Not to judge, not to prod, not to change;
to observe.

There is no technique for this,
only a subtle mode of consciousness;
an in-sight directly sensing
the holiness of things as they are in the "is" without the
    "ism."

Meditation is not learned, but lived.
Only when trying stops does doing begin.
Only when thoughts cease does in-sight commence.

In-sight originates with Universe,
and is received by us
only when we observe ourselves and our world with
    attentive minds.

Meditation is a transfusion of wisdom
from Ocean to wave, from Whole to part,
bypassing our thoughtful presuppositions
as a blood transfusion bypasses the heart.

Meditation is a direct seeing into the suchness of things,
involving the seer in a radical transformation
from self to Self, wave to Ocean, I to God.

LIFE

Life is the unfolding
of the actual from the potential.

Life is the ON of Universe
spinning between two OFFs,
themselves vibrating between two ONs.

No illusion,
no mirrored image of a greater something,
Life is all there is
at the moment there is anything at all.

Life embraces its own negation;
ON precipitates OFF,
and is in turn precipitated by it.

Life cannot be clung to
as if it existed outside oneself.
It cannot be transformed
as if it could be other than it is at the moment it is.

Life cannot be conquered,
or mastered,
or martyred.
It can only be lived.

FOREVER NAMELESS

Let me affirm the Name that is forever Nameless;
Let me affirm the One who is also the Many;
Let me know in my heart that You are not bound
by a thing or its opposite,
a name or a label;
Let me know in my heart
that You are not other than what Is,
that beclouded unknowing
shimmering just beyond the eye of Ism.

DOUBTS

The doubts won't let me go;
they hammer and pound,
shattering the thickest wall.
The damage
sometimes lasts generations.
Yet there are moments
brief, elusive,
when the doubts scatter;
my vision clears
and I know
that the doubts,

too,

make me

who I am.

MORNING

Is it morning,

really morning,

or is it just

another day?

A new beginning

or just a continuing yesterday?

How I wish for morning:

a soft light

bleaching a night's pain.

A new beginning,

a new day.

But I fear morning's no longer with me.

Beginnings rarely seek me out—

I am too much with middles.

MIRROR OF ALL

Today I stand before the Mirror of All
to see myself as I am.
I come with no gifts, no bribes, no illusions, no excuses.
I stand without defense and wait to be filled.
What will fill me?
Remorse, certainly.
So much error and needless pain.
And joy: remembered moments of love and right doing.
I am too complex for single-sided emotions.
And I am too simple to be excused by my complexity.
Let me be bold enough to see,
humble enough to feel,
daring enough to turn and
embrace the way of justice, mercy, and simplicity.

SOURCE OF ALL

You are the Source of all.
From You comes light and from You comes darkness.
From You comes peace and from You comes strife.
All that is awesome and all that is awful have their roots in
    You.
And so do I.

How frightening to know that

the One who lifts the dark and prepares the dawn, dwells
within me as well.

I tremble knowing I am a part of You.

You speak and there is order.

You speak and there is chaos.

And I am in Your image.

I, too, speak and create order and chaos.

My words also heal and hurt.

Take care of Your world, my Love, as I will strive to take care
of mine.

GOOD AND EVIL

Oh, to believe in the Good as if Evil were an illusion.

Oh, to seek refuge in a God who shows only love.

Then would I hide from the world and seek only You.

Then would I turn from the pain and rest secure in the inner
pockets of Your peace.

But You are not such a god.

"Behold I place before you life and death, blessing and curse"—

For every joy there is a sorrow.

For every uplift there is a slide.

The one embraces the other and neither stands alone:

Life and death, blessing and curse;

seeming opposites united in a greater whole.

I cannot pretend to eternal peace when there is so much pain.

I cannot hope for detached calm when my world swirls in torrents about me.

And yet I turn to You.

To You, the Source of my torment and my triumphs.

To You, the One who holds back nothing and offers me all.

You are my Source and my Substance.

From You all things come, in You all things arise, to You all things return.

You are the eternal play of birth, death, and rebirth.

And yet You are more than the impersonal,

You are also the Way: the way of justice, mercy, and simplicity.

For all the hardships of life still there is a way to live:

doing justly, loving mercy, living simply, walking humbly,

attending to the ordinary with courtesy and grace.

I live in a vast and wild world. May I learn to live in it well.

DO I MATTER?

Standing before the One who is all the world,
can it be that I matter?
Can it be that such a small thing as me
has a place in such a grand scheme?
And yet it is so.

I am empty of permanence.
I don't endure.
My days are limited and too few to fulfill the desires of my
    heart.
I am so small and temporary. And yet so important.

This pile of dust speaks!
This bag of skin thinks!
This frail body acts and makes a difference!

I am the only me that has ever been.
I am shaken by the knowledge that
I never existed before and will not again.

The Source rebirths, but never repeats.
Infinite possibility demands infinite diversity.

Whatever I must do I must do here and now.
Whatever gift I am to give I must give it here and now.
Whatever purpose I am to fulfill I must fulfill it here and now.

I am what I am here and now.
I am what I do with who I am.

REMEMBERING

When I replay the year now closing,
my heart shivers.
I have caused much pain.

Through thoughtlessness and inconsideration,
through wanton disregard for the feelings of others,
I have left many I love feeling unloved.

Oh, I had my reasons.
But what once was so clearly right is now but clouded excuse.
I must amend the past and start anew.

I vow this day
to speak more softly,
to do more carefully,
to be more fully what I know I am capable of being:
a friend, a lover, a caregiver, and guide.

I vow this day to challenge my own excuses,
that I give more of myself and less to my selfishness.

Inscribe me in the Book of Life for the sake of Life,
that by my life I might enrich Life.

HERE I AM

Here I am.
A little nervous, a bit self conscious
standing here before . . . whom?
Myself? My God? My peers?
To whom shall I report and
from whom shall I seek guidance?

Am I strong enough to judge myself?
Am I so sure of me that I can listen to You?
Am I so evil or so good as to merit this season of introspection?
And yet here I am.

Oh, there are things I would change.
Little things mostly. Simple things.

It wouldn't be hard to be a bit more caring, attentive, nurturing.
It wouldn't be hard to make myself more the person I pretend
    to be.

Pretense. Maybe that's what this is all about.
Who have I fooled this past year? And who have I failed to fool?
Who knows me, and how do I treat one who knows?

Yes, there is room to change. To grow. To mature.
Yes, there is a prayer to utter, even if I am not sure I believe . . .
What shall I pray?
Just this: Let no one be put to shame because of me.

Oh, I have much to do.

WHAT I AM GIVEN

"Choose life, that you and your children may live."
—Deuteronomy 30:15, 19

I've been given the gift of mind, the blessing of reason and
imagination.
But too often I use logic to excuse evil and fancy to mask
wickedness.

I've been given the gift of sight, the blessing of seeing the
world's beauty.
But too often I focus only on myself.

I've been given the gift of hearing: I can listen to the rushing
stream,
the howling wind, the crashing sea, the solitary bird, the new-
born's cry.
But too often I'm deaf to all but my own complaining.

I've been given the gift of speech, song, and prayer.
I can whisper words of love and argue loudly for justice.
But too often I turn away from right speech and indulge in
gossip, lies, and half-truths.

I've been given the gift of hands: to caress, to hold, to build.
But too often I grasp and strangle and destroy.

I've been given the gift of Life and the blessing of creating life.
I can raise children and teach them.

But too often I discount the gift, imagining there's some-
thing more important.

Too often I'm content to give birth when I must also give
Life.

What shall I say to excuse my errors?

What shall I say to erase deeds that should not have been
done?

The past is fixed, only the present is fluid.

Shall I choose Life? Or shall I simply excuse my living?

WALKING ON

I call You,
my beginning and my end,
my destiny and my destination,
that I might find within myself
and among my friends
the power to heal broken hearts.

May neither death nor sorrow triumph over me.

May I comfort those who mourn,
and give strength and consolation to those in pain.

May I learn to cherish what is eternal,
the fleeting now,
this very moment of meeting and embrace.

GIFTS GIVEN

(Written in honor of child organ donors)

To save a single life is to save an entire world.
—Talmud

Each of us comes into this world
as a gift . . . bearing gifts . . . being gifts.
Each of us comes into this world
with a purpose . . . bearing meaning . . . being meaning.
Tell me—please!—why this suffering;
why this awful burden searing my heart
with a fire only love can survive . . . survive but not soothe.
There is no soothing in this pain;
No comfort in this loss;
No meaning in this mindless swirl of terror and tears.
There is only the numbing that accompanies
the ragged-edged hardness of
life's too swift unfolding.
And yet the gift remains.
The moments shared and anticipated.
The dream lived and dreamt anew.
The gift remains.
And with it the obligation—
making this world a little better for our having been here.
No matter how long or short the sojourn,

no matter even if the eyes never open nor the lungs fill with
   air,
still the obligation remains.
How to meet it?
We meet it in death as we should meet it in life:
By giving the gift that each of us is.
By lending to others what has been lent to us: the gift of Life.
In the midst of our pain we call out
to the One who establishes all things.
Feel my anguish as the decision is made.
Comfort me with the knowing that
the way of this gift is the right way,
the way of compassion,
the way of service,
the way of caring,
the way of Life.
Give me the courage to give the gift.
Grant me the strength to live with the giving.
Open my heart to the Presence
that knocks so softly at my soul's gate, whispering: Give . . .
To save a single life is to save an entire world.
May this world that is about to die embrace only peace.
May the world about to be saved embrace only love.
May the world that is about to be shattered know in time
the tender touch of healing.
The gift has been given.
May it be for a blessing.

TURNINGS

I marvel at seasons' turning,
at moment's dying and birthing.
I marvel at change
and gape at surprise.
But oh how it scares me
this ever new wonder I call ordinary.
How I long for sameness,
for consistency,
for just one expectation met
as I imagine it to be met.
But frightened wishes
cannot make a world,
only color it—with fear, with anguish,
with fanatic lunging after illusions of control
when in fact all there is is only this:
our wild and turning world.

CALLINGS

I am called as a lover calls the beloved.
The sky calls to me, and the earth;
the wind whispers my name
and trees rustle with secret embrace.

Arise my love, my fair one, and come away—
away from the fear of being alone;
away from the fear of being too close;
away from the fear of being the same;
away from the fear of being different;
away from the fear of being loved;
away from the fear of being unloved;
away from the fear of being yourself;
away from the fear of being someone else.

PEACE PRAYER

We call upon the Source and Substance of all reality,
to open our bodies, hearts, and minds to the divine manifest
   in and as all beings.

We pray for peace: peace in our hearts, peace in our homes,
   peace in our communities, for only in this way can we
   make peace in the world.

We pray for the safety of combatants and noncombatants
   alike. May they see in each other not friend or foe, but
   fellow humans sharing a commonality truer and deeper
   than the surface differences we mistake for ontological
   divisions.

We pray for spaciousness of mind
to know that diversity is divinity manifest in time and space.

We pray for spaciousness of heart
to know that love is greater than fear.

We pray for the humility
to know we do not know.

We pray for the courage to question our certainties.

We pray for the strength to put down our prejudices.

We pray for the clarity to see in the other the infinitely
faceted Face of God.

We pray for the grace to awaken to the truth of One God,
One Humanity, One World, and One Moral Code: justice
and compassion for all.

May each of us attend to the deepest and best within us
that we might weave the diverse and unique threads of our
lives
into a universal tapestry of wisdom, kindness, and peace.

We ask for this in all Your Names: those we know and those
we do not; those we can speak and those we cannot;
those we remember and those we have forgotten; those
we are taught and those we have yet to learn; and in that
Great Name beyond naming: the silence that embraces
all things in wonder.

RENEWAL

Imagine not that life is all dong.
Stillness, too, is life;
And in that stillness
The mind cluttered with busyness quiets,
The heart reaching to win rests,
And we hear the whispered truths of God.

TWILIGHT

Bless the One
Who spins day into dusk.
With wisdom watch
The dawn gates open;
With understanding let
Time and seasons
Come and go;
With awe perceive
The stars in lawful orbit.
Morning dawns,
Evening darkens;
Darkness and light yielding
One to the other,
Yet each distinguished
And unique.

Marvel at Life!
Strive to know her ways!
Seek wisdom and truth,
The gateways to life's mysteries.
Wondrous indeed
Is the evening twilight.

CAUSELESS LOVE

The threat to our salvation is the clash of peoples—
Jews and Arabs,
Offspring of a single father,
Separated in youth by jealousy,
In adolescence by fear,
In adulthood by power,
In old age by habit.
It is time to break these habits of hate
And create new habits:
Habits of the heart
That will awake within us the causeless love of redemption
    and peace.

CONDUIT TO GOD

Sing and awake.
Sing the never-before-sung.
Sing a new song
To God
From God
As God.
I still my mind and calm my heart;
I soften my breath and fill my belly with air;
I hold that fullness in tension
To be released only when the spirit moves.
My breath is transformed
From silence to sound,
From mystery to music and
Back to mystery again.
For breath is the conduit to God,
And song the sound of breath in love.

DANCE OF GOD

Like a wave arising from the ocean's dance,
So do we arise from the dance of God.
Like a wave returning from the rocky shore,
Its form given to chaos,
But its essence restored in the ocean's unity,
So do we return from life's end
Recycled in holiness
To dance once more.
Awesome and wondrous is the Dance of God.

RETURN

I acknowledge before the Source of all
That life and death are not in my hands.
May it come to pass that I be healed,
But if death is my fate
Then I accept it with dignity
And the loving calm of one who knows the way of all things.
May my death be honorable,
May my life be a healing memory for those who know me.
May my loved ones think well of me
And may my memory bring them joy.

From all those I may have hurt,

I ask forgiveness.

Upon all those who have hurt me,

I bestow forgiveness.

As a wave returns to the ocean,

So I return to the Source from which I came.

I CHOOSE YOU

I choose you this day to love and confide in,

To hold on to and reach out from.

I choose you this day

To believe in and to share with,

To learn from and to grow with.

I choose you this day to give you my heart.

BLESS THIS FRIENDSHIP

Bless this friendship:

May it be as deep and wondrous as any love can be,

And may it lead these lovers beyond themselves

Into the broader circle of friendship and peace.

SHARING A MEAL

We give thanks to the Power that makes for meeting,
For our table has been a place of dialogue and friendship.
We give thanks to life.
May we never lose touch with the simple joy and wonder
    of sharing a meal.

ON THE ADOPTION OF A CHILD

We are humbled by the awesome responsibility of this moment.
We are filled with joy and trembling
As we contemplate the tasks that lie before us:
Modeling love, teaching courage,
Instilling honesty, integrity, and responsibility.
May we come to embody the virtues we teach,
And may our children see in us
The values and behaviors we hope to see in them.

LIGHTING THE HANUKKAH CANDLES

We kindle this light in honor of hope:
May we never lose heart in our quest for justice.
We kindle this light in honor of action:
May we never mistake wishing for doing.
We kindle this light in honor of nature:
May our eyes never dim to her wonders
nor our ears grow deaf to her cries of pain.
We kindle this light in honor of unity:
May we celebrate our differences,
and yet have the courage to see beyond them.
We kindle this light in honor of knowledge:
May we free ourselves from opinion
that we might open ourselves to truth.
We kindle this light in honor of kindness:
May we cultivate compassion in thought, word, and deed.
We kindle this light in honor of heroism:
May we never surrender to tyranny no matter how dear
    we hold the tyrant.

ANNIVERSARY BLESSING

"When husband and wife love each other as they love themselves, honor each other more than they honor themselves, and guide their children in the right path, Torah says of them: You shall know they dwell in peace."
—*Yevamot 62b*

When you first entered into the covenant of love,
You sought to maintain your uniqueness as individuals
While enhancing your integrity as a couple.
This ideal is hard to maintain.
Too often we yield our integrity, and
Sacrifice our creativity.
We call this compromise,
But it is more often surrender.

In the short term, it appears easier;
In the long term it spells disaster.
The marriage you seek
Knows not surrender but dialogue,
Not victors and vanquished
But mutuality, meeting, and honest struggle.

At this anniversary of your marriage
We wish for you the blessings
Of integrity and integration,
Of joy and happiness,
Of purpose and peace.

May you renew your commitment each to the other
That your lives be blessings unto you both.

GOD

The One who is the many
The Ocean who is the wave
The Puzzle who is the piece
Is God
The whole and holy.

THE ROUND OF BEING

God is holiness giving rise to creation.
God is creation giving rise to consciousness.
God is consciousness giving rise to self.
God is self giving rise to non-self.
God is no-self giving rise to holiness.
God is holiness . . .
I praise the great round of Being
And give thanks for the blessings
That come to me each day.

ONE WITHOUT END

Before the birth of becoming
There was the Source of Being.
When all is ended, that Source remains.
Alone without second, the One is all.
This One is my God, my redeemer, my refuge, my shelter.
This One is the cup of life from which I drink daily.
When I wake, as when I sleep, I rest in This.
One Substance in infinite manifestation,
One mind in infinite variation.
Know this and fear not.

FOR THE GIFTS WE RECEIVE

For the Gift of Sleep

Blessed are You, Comforting One, Who gifts my eyes with
sleep.

For the Gift of Dream

Blessed are You, Weaver of Dreams, Whose symbols point
me toward wholeness.

For the Gift of Washing the Hands

Blessed are You, Source of all doing, Who reminds me to
act with clean hands.

For the Gift of a Healthy Body

Blessed are You, Source and Substance of all Who fashions
   me with wisdom.

You bless me with a body of wondrous balance and
   complexity

that opens and closes in tune with need and necessity.

If openings should close or that which is closed open
   improperly,

I could not endure.

I honor Your gift by honoring my body and respecting its
   promise.

Blessed are You, Healer of all flesh,

Who blesses me with form and function.

For the Gift of Waking Up

Blessed are You, Awakened One,

Who awakens my mind to the pure breath of Your essence.

For the Gift of a Discerning Mind

Blessed are You, the One and the Many,

Who gives me the capacity to honor the play of opposites.

For the Gift of Seeking

Blessed are You, the Pathless One, Who offers each a path
   to truth.

For the Gift of Freedom

Blessed are You, the Boundless One, Whose Way is the way
   of freedom.

For the Gift of Gender

Blessed are You, the Imageless One, Who fashions male and female in Your image.

For the Gift of Clarity

Blessed are You, the All-Seeing, Who opens the blind eye.

For the Gift of Clothing

Blessed are You, Sustainer of life, Who clothes the naked.

For the Gift of Movement

Blessed are You, Source of all Change, Who releases the bound.

For the Gift of Simplicity

Blessed are You, the Everpresent One, Who untangles the knotted.

For the Gift of Solid Ground

Blessed are You, Ground of Being, Who spreads out dry land in the midst of the sea.

For the Gift of Sustenance

Blessed are You, Source of all Life, Who provides for all my needs.

For the Gift of Walking

Blessed are You, the Way and Its Walker, Who prepares my every step.

For the Gift of Strength

Blessed are You, Fearless One, Who makes for courage.

For the Gift of Wonder

Blessed are You, Source of Wonder, Who opens me to the glory of creation.

For the Gift of Renewal

Blessed are You, Fountain of Being, Who revives me in moments of exhaustion.

For the Gift of Wakefulness

Blessed are You, Awakened One, Who removes sleep from my eyes.

For the Gift of Learning

Blessed are You, Giver of Wisdom, Who sanctifies me in Your service
With the opportunity to immerse myself in truth.

For the Gift of Wisdom

Blessed are You, Giver of Wisdom, Who sweetens wisdom in our mouths.

The Gift of Creation

Blessed are You, Source of Life, Who creates the world from the vibration of Your words.

For the Gift of Love

Blessed are You, Beloved, Who loves us with an endless love.

For the Gift of Redemption

Blessed are You, Bringer of Hope, Who redeems us from folly, evil, and slavery.

For the Gift of the Night

Blessed are You, Bringer of Shadows, Who brings on evening
with a word.

For the Gift of Morning

Blessed are You, Source of all turning, Who grants me the
opportunity of a new day.

For the Gift of Eternal Love

Blessed are You, Beloved, Whose love is without duration.

For the Gift of Seeing Natural Wonders

Blessed are You, Source of all Life, Who fashions nature
with breathtaking wonder.

For the Gift of Receiving a Miracle

Blessed are You, Source of Salvation, Who aided me in a
moment of need.

For the Gift of Hearing Good News

Blessed are You, Source of Joy, Who allows me to rejoice in
this moment.

For the Gift of Hearing Very Bad News

Blessed are You, Source of Sorrow, Who allows me to share
the pain of the world.

For the Gift of the New, Honoring the Moment

Blessed are You, Timeless One of Being,
from Whom I arise, in Whom I live,
and with Whom I awake to the glory of this moment.

A PRAYER FOR OUR WARRIORS

Dear God,

We come into Your Presence to ask

for the welfare of our loved ones fighting around the globe.

Let them feel Your Presence as we pray they can feel ours.

Let them draw upon Your Strength as we pray they can draw

upon ours.

Let them know in You the simple truths for which they fight:

justice, kindness, respect, and honor.

Be their Father and rest Your Hand upon their shoulders.

Be their Mother and rest their heads in Your arms.

Be their Oasis that they may find these moments of rest.

Be their Shield and protect their spirits even as they place

their bodies in harm's way.

Yet do not shield them from the horror of war,

but use that horror to awaken their love for peace.

Dear God,

We cannot ask for the safety of some

and not ask for the safety of all.

We cannot plead for the homecoming of one

and not ask that all return home whole and well.

We cannot yearn for our own only;

we must and we do yearn for the peace of all.

May You Who make peace throughout the heavens

make for peace among the children of Abraham,

Hagar, and Sarah.

May they see in each other the One Who is all.
And may they honor their common father by doing as he
   did,
opening their tents wide to welcome the stranger and
   discover a friend.

PREPARING TO MARRY

It is impossible to grow up in a family without
pain, hurt, and anguish.
It is impossible for one human being
to intimately care for another without experiencing
both the deepest angers as well as fathomless love.
As we are about to blend ourselves into a new harmony,
it is incumbent upon us
to blanket ourselves in peace and forgiveness.

Let us open our hearts to the joy of love.
Let the glimmer of past joys
kindle the fires of present wonder
and let us embrace one another in forgiveness.

> If I have hurt you in any way,
> advertently or inadvertently,
> consciously or unconsciously,
> I ask for your forgiveness.

We are about to enter into a unique covenant,
a bond of body, mind, and spirit.
We acknowledge the hurts that are to come
and pledge to keep our hearts forever open to healing.
We welcome the joys that are to come
and vow to keep our hearts forever open to wonder.
We acknowledge the complexities of life alone and together,
and promise to keep our hearts forever open to forgiveness.

TRUE UNION

There are three things too wonderful for me;
Yea, four I cannot fathom, I cannot see;
The way of an eagle in the air,
The way of a serpent upon a rock,
The way of a ship in the midst of the sea,
And the way of a man with a woman
and a woman with a man. (Proverbs 30)

The way of men and women.
Struggling with self and other, the I and the not-I,
seeking that elusive shadow within
sometimes by aimlessly wandering without.
But the work of a spouse
is not to be the shadow of the other,
but to help the other be who that person truly is.

We tend to seek out reflections of ourselves to love
and are sorely troubled when the other person
fails to mirror our needs, our desires, and our truths.
But true union begins when we look
beyond the mirror of self-absorption
to see who we have met on his or her own terms.

THE SEVEN BLESSINGS
(adapted from the Jewish wedding service)

Blessed is the Source of Life, the Fountain of all being,
by whose power fruit comes forth from the vine.
Blessed is the Source of Life, the Fountain of all being,
whose glory pervades all creation.
Blessed is the Source of Life, the Fountain of all being,
whose essence is the essence of humankind,
and who bestowed upon us the gift of creation
that we might heal our world with justice and peace.
Let us rejoice in the Divine Mystery whose nature is revealed
in the passion and love of bridegroom and bride.
And let us bless this friendship;
may it be as deep and wondrous as any love can be,
and may it lead these lovers beyond themselves
into the broader circle of friendship and peace.

Blessed is the Source of Life, the Fountain of all being,

whose secret is found in the rejoicing of bridegroom and
bride.

Blessed is the Source of Life, the Fountain of all being,

whose power gives rise to joy and gladness, bride and groom,
mirth and song,

love and harmony, pleasure and delight, peace and
companionship.

Soon may we hear in all our homes and all our communities,

in every city and throughout all nations,

the voice of joy and gladness,

the voice of bride and groom,

the jubilant voices of people feasting with song.

Let this day of union be also a day of reunion.

Let each of us take up the challenge of companionship

that all the world be joined in friendship and love,

and all peoples come together in a harmony of differences

beneath the divine *chuppah* [canopy] of peace.

GIFTS

I have been given the gift of mind, the blessing of reason
and imagination,

But too often I use logic to excuse evil and fancy to mask
wickedness.

I have been given the gift of sight,

But too often I focus solely on my self.

I have been given the gift of hearing,

But too often I am deaf to all but my own complaining.

I have been given the gift of speech, song, and prayer,

But too often I wallow in gossip, lies, and propaganda.

I have been given the gift of hands that I might caress, hold,
and build,

But too often I use them simply to grasp, strangle, and destroy.

BLESSING GOD

How can we bless God when God is the Source of all blessing?

When we bless God we tap that Source of blessing

And open our hearts to the wonder of creation.

When we bless God

We do not add to the majesty of the One

But repair our attitude toward the Many.

We do not so much praise the Creator

As raise the Creation.

To bless God is to welcome life

And embrace the turmoil of being

with the light of our becoming.

ALL IN EACH

All in each:
The one in the many
the I in the Thou;
Each completing the other:
Day and night
Desert and sea
Fire and water
Earth and sky;
So simple, so subtle—
It escapes me time and again,
And yet for a moment I glimpse the thread
That weaves me with you.
For a moment I am not—we are.
And I bend the knee in silent wonder
And cry and laugh and embrace the world.

YOU ARE MY ENEMY

You are my enemy; you whom I love so much;
You around whom I spread my dreams like blankets
To keep out the night's chill.
You are my enemy:
The enemy of my lies

My screams

My tears that rush to extinguish the guilt burning in the
    ashes of your pain.

You are my enemy:

The enemy of my drama

My games

My confusions that twist the obvious into the dubious.

You are my enemy.

With you I live.

Without you I am already dead.

CREATED TO SERVE

To serve God is to serve life,

To nurture her with reason and compassion.

To bond with holiness is to recognize

The unity of all things

And to act toward others

As you would act toward yourself

For indeed they are yourself.

A PARABLE

· · · · · · · · · · · · · · · · ·

Reenvisioning the Book of Job

A PARABLE:
REENVISIONING THE
BOOK OF JOB

. . .

Much of my work is a recasting of ancient text. My goal is to help you hear what I hear when I read these texts in their original language, and in this way to invite you to consider new understandings of these old works. This is no less true of my retelling of the Book of Job. While the Book of Job is far longer than the psalms and poems collected in this volume, and while my reworking of the story is a more radical reimagining, the story of Job and the questions it raises about the nature of God and justice are so central to my thinking, and so primed to challenge you to think as well, that I offer it here as icing on what I hope is a delicious dark chocolate cake of poetic exploration.

ACT ONE, Scene One

Satan [*dressed in a black tuxedo and standing in front of a stage curtain, he speaks to the audience*]:
I'm God's *sahtahn*, His prosecuting attorney.
My job is to fly around your planet and report back on
    what I find.
The usual stuff mostly:
child abuse, spousal abuse,
a Qur'an burning here, a church burning there,
and religious folk killing other folk in the Name of God.
Not the Real God, of course. He doesn't actually have a
    Name.
People just make up gods so they can kill people
or damn them or just to feel superior to them.
Whatever.
Mostly God just shrugs it off—puny humans and all that.
But every once in a while though . . .
[*trails off thoughtfully as the curtain rises and we are in heaven*]

ACT ONE, Scene Two

[In heaven, God, dressed in a white tuxedo and sitting on a La-Z-Boy recliner. Satan walks into the scene and approaches God.]

God *[happily calling Satan over]*: You've been checking things
   out on earth?
Did you notice my boy, Job?
Man I love that guy.
He prays to me all day long.
He even prays to Me on behalf of his kids,
just in case they forget to pray to Me, which,
of course, they never do.
There is no one like Job on the whole planet.
That guy loves me.

Satan *[scornfully]*: Of course he loves you;
you've given him everything a guy like him could want:
a good marriage, great kids, a thriving business, sound
   health.
What's not to love?
Knock him down a peg, and I bet he'll curse you to your
   face.

God *[excitedly]*: A bet?

You want to bet me that Job will curse me if I batter him
   around a bit?

What's in it for Me?

Satan: Bragging rights.

God: I've got everything else,

and you can't beat bragging rights.

What's in it for you?

Satan: I get some relief from You always asking me

if I've seen your great friend Job.

I get sick and tired of Your smug . . .

God: OK, you're on! One condition though:

don't damage Job himself;

do what you want to what he has,

but not to who he is,

and let's see if he curses me or not.

ACT ONE, Scene Three

[*In Job's dining room. There are two doors leading into the room, one at the far end away from Job, the other behind him. Job is having a snack by himself. Satan sits off in a corner "invisible" to Job. Satan snaps his fingers, and Servant One, wearing a tattered and bloody robe, bursts into the room from one of the doors and rushes up to Job.*]

Servant One: My Lord Job!
The Sabeans have attacked your cattle!
They slew all the men and stole the cows.
I alone escaped to tell you!

[*Before he finishes speaking, Satan snaps his fingers again, and Servant Two, wearing a tattered and burnt and smoldering robe, bursts through the other door and rushes up to Job.*]

Servant Two: My Lord Job!
Lightening struck the sheep pens!
The entire herd was consumed in flame, even the shepherds
    lit up like torches.
I alone escaped to tell you!

[*Before he finishes speaking, Satan snaps his fingers again, and Servant Three, wearing a torn robe with arrows sticking through it, bursts through the first door and races up to Job.*]

Servant Three: My Lord Job!

Chaldeans attacked your caravan!

They stole all your goods along with your herd of camels.

They slew everyone!

I alone escaped to tell you!

[Before he finishes speaking, Satan snaps his fingers again, and Servant Four, dressed in a robe filthy with dust and covered in stone chips, bursts through the first door and races up to Job.]

Servant Four: My Lord Job!

Your sons and daughters were feasting together

when a windstorm blew through the hall,

collapsing it, and killing them all!

I alone escaped to tell you!

[The servants encircle Job crying, "My Lord Job! My Lord Job!" Job is disoriented. This prefigures God swirling around Job later in the story. Satan watches from the corner eager to see Job curse God.]

Satan *[to himself]*: Come on! Come on! Curse Him already!

Job *[Suddenly, Job screams and silences the servants. Tearing his robe in agony, he cries wordlessly.]*

Satan [*to himself*]: OK, here it comes. I knew he'd fold. I
  know my humans.

Job: Naked I came from my mother's womb
and naked will I return.
God gives, God takes—blessed be the Name of God!

Satan [*furious that Job didn't curse God*]: Blessed be the—
what does it take to shake this idiot?

God [*Appearing to Satan but invisible to Job and the servants,
    God says gleefully*]:
I win! I win! I told you he wouldn't curse Me!
Job is a saint. Bragging rights are Mine!

Satan [*caustically*]: Of course he didn't curse you.
You did a number on his cows, sheep, and kids,
but rattle his body and bones a bit
and I bet he'll curse You to Your face.

God: Another bet? After I crushed you with this one?
  What's in it for Me?

Satan: Just knowing that I'm wrong,
and that the guy really loves.
That is what You want most, isn't it?
That people love You for who You are not what You can
  give them?

God: It's true.

I command them to love Me,

and then wonder if they really do or if they are just afraid
 not to.

I mean, I command them to love Me,

and then I demand that they do so freely,

but that is somewhat oxymoronic.

Satan *[sarcastically]*: Somewhat? It's impossible.

You can't command someone to do something of their own
 free will.

God: But who really knows?

Satan: What do You mean, who really knows?

I just explained it to You.

You know, that's why You keep testing these people.

You don't trust them.

But this time with this guy

You just might learn what You so desperately want to
 know:

does he really love You or not?

God *[wistfully]*: Won't that be great . . .

[excitedly] OK! You're on! Just don't kill him,

otherwise we won't know who wins.

[God disappears, and the servants exit, leaving Job alone with his grief. Satan snaps his fingers one last time; suddenly Job is covered head to toe with oozing sores. Job's wife enters by one of the doors. Seeing her husband covered in sores, she screams.]

Job's Wife: How much more can you endure? Curse God and die already!

Satan *[to himself]*: Now you're talking.

Job *[speaking to his wife with difficulty]*: Are you crazy?
We welcomed the good from God;
surely we can accept the evil as well.

Job's Wife: I'm crazy?
You're the one bursting with puss and praising the Lord.
God's playing with you like He plays with all of us.
Just put an end to it.

Job *[more to convince himself than his wife, he starts to chant in order to drown out his wife's words]*: God is good. God is great. God is just. God has a plan.
Praise Him! Praise Him! Let every sore praise Him!
God is good. God is great. God is just. God has a plan.
Praise Him! Praise Him! Let every sore praise Him!

Satan *[to himself]*: Idiot.

ACT TWO, Scene One

[Eliphaz, Bildad, and Zophar, Job's three best friends, arrive at his home to comfort him. Job is sitting outside on a low wooden crate, and as they draw near they see him and tear their robes in grief.]

Job: God is good. God is great. God is just. God has a plan.
Praise Him! Praise Him! Let every sore praise Him!
God is good. God is great. God is just. God has a plan.
Praise Him! Praise Him! Let every sore praise Him!

Eliphaz to the other two: Look at him!
I thought he was beyond reproach . . .
God doesn't do this to the good.

Bildad to the other two: So much for all that hype
about his impeachable integrity.
God doesn't do this to the just.

Zophar to the other two: Man, were we wrong.
Job must have done something horrible to deserve this.
Maybe we shouldn't associate with him at all.
Do you think his sins are catching?

[All three friends look at each other, then shake their heads. The three friends walk into Job's yard, pull up crates of their own from the yard, and sit with Job in silence. Job ignores them for a bit. Then he says softly:]

Job: Look at me, brothers. Look at what I have become.

I hate my life!

Better I was never born than to be burdened with this evil.

Better they had pulled me from my mother's womb and
  drowned me in a lake. Better they had fed me poison
  than the milk of my mother's breast.

I sit here and chew on my suffering like a dog sucking the
  grizzle from a bone.

My worst fears have happened; my nightmares are real.

All I want is to die, and instead I am cursed to live.

What is God trying to teach me with this evil?

Eliphaz: God? Evil?

Listen, Job, stuff like this happens for a reason.

The innocent don't suffer like this;

this kind of thing is reserved for the guilty.

Don't blame your mother, or our God;

this is your fault.

Confess your guilt and repent, and God will end this
  horror.

If I were you, I'd pray to God and admit my sins,

and trust Him to forgive you.

Job [*to Eliphaz*]: My sins? What sins?

And my prayer goes unanswered: [*sarcastically*]

"Dear God, Great God, Almighty God—kill me!"

I have no sins, and He has no response.

And who the hell are you to accuse me of sin?

Tell me one time I failed you, or *[turning to the others]* either
of you?

One time! No, not even once?

I'm a good man, and my suffering is pointless.

And now you *[looking at Eliphaz]* accuse me?

[scoffingly Job spits up blood on the ground] My sin my ass!

Bildad: Shut up!

We didn't come here to listen to this garbage!

If you didn't sin, certainly your kids did.

Why else would God kill them?

Are you saying God treats the good no better than the
wicked?

Nonsense!

Do good, get good—that's the way God does it.

Do bad, get bad—that's the way of God.

All we have to do is look at you to know your claims of
innocence are a lie.

God doesn't torture the good!

Job *[to Bildad]*: I know that's what we say,

and I know that's how this looks, but I'm guilty of nothing.

I can't prove my innocence,

but I refuse to confess to something I haven't done.

I'm not covering up for anything, or denying anything.

All I want is justice.

I demand justice!

Isn't that what God demands? Should we ask for less?

If I knew how, I would stand before God and say,

"You have treated me unjustly.

You have caused me to loathe life.

Is this what we can expect from You?

Punish me if I'm guilty, but why kill my children?

Bring me to justice, sure, but dare first to tell me of what I
    am being charged.

Or do You punish first, and seek reasons later?"

Zophar [to Job]: Blasphemer! That alone dooms you.

Your suffering proves your guilt; your blathering only
    compounds it.

God knows you're a sinner, and now the whole world
    knows it as well.

Everyone is talking:

"Have you heard about Job? Lying son of a bitch.

All this time pretending to be Mr. Holy,

when in fact he is worse than the rest of us combined.

Damn him for making me feel small.

But God is good, and the bastard is getting his due."

But you can still save your reputation—

confess your sin and God will forgive you,

and people will respect you once again.

We all love the repentant sinner.

Job: And you are my friends? And this is how you
   comfort me?

With gossip and accusations and stupid clichés?

I know God can do whatever He wants,

and for some reason He wants to torment me.

But I don't have to make excuses for Him.

If anyone is to be held to account, it ought to be God.

Let God appear before me and explain Himself.

Let Him accuse me or heal me and accuse Himself.

Eliphaz *[to Job]*: Shut up! Just shut up, you fool.

God is going to come to you? Apologize to you? Explain
   Himself to you?

Who do you think you are?

Job *[to Eliphaz]*: Listen you gas bag, is this how you
   comfort me?

Maybe I should speak aloud your sins.

[Eliphaz shudders and spits on the ground angrily.]

Maybe my suffering is just a way for God to bring you here

so that we can see what a heartless friend *you* really are!

*[Job stops, looks at the ground, kicks the dirt, sighs, and composes
   himself.]*

But I'm not going to condemn you.

I'm not even angry at you.

It's God who makes me angry.

It's God I want to talk to. It's God whom I charge with
    injustice.

Bildad [to Job]: Whoa! Let's be careful what we ask for.
The last thing I want is for God to show up.
If that's your plan, I'm going home.
We all know the fate of the wicked, and you are living it.
Curse us all you want, but we know the face of justice and
    this is it:
your lies have been exposed and your wickedness is being
    punished,
and I for one am glad of it.
Your pain confirms my faith.
The godless are shut off in darkness, and you, my friend,
are just one small step from the pit.
Confess and repent before it's too late!

Job [to Bildad]: Your comfort [sarcastically] only compounds
    my suffering.
You want to believe in a mad God who terrorizes the
    innocent? Fine.
You want to call this madness truth? Fine.
You want to blame me for His cruelty? Fine.
But don't expect me to listen to it and, even worse,
to justify it by confessing to things I've never done.
No, run home if you wish, Bildad,
but I want God to show Himself! I want to plead my case in
    His Court.

Zophar *[to Job]*: Listen to yourself,
demanding of God that which we humans cannot even
    demand of ourselves.
Justice? You've had justice:
God gave you everything only to steal it back.
He raised you up only to throw you down.
My only regret is that we didn't realize His plan,
and believed your success was a blessing from God
rather than a setup to make your suffering all the more
    painful for you.
The evil you endure is the evil you deserve.
If Bildad and Eliphaz and I deserve any blame,
it's for loving you so much
that we ignored how evil you really are.

Job *[to the three friends]*: The three of you are fools,
worshiping a god of your own imagining,
one who excuses your own wickedness.
My God may be callous, but yours is cruel.
I *am* the man you thought I was:
generous to the poor, supportive of the powerless,
never rejoicing in another's pain, even those who schemed
    against me.
I was trustworthy in business,
and reliable as a husband, father, and friend.
I was, I *am*, the man you now say I only pretended to be.
And why do you say this?

Because you insist on worshiping a fantasy of a just God
rather than accepting the reality of a mad God.
I don't doubt there is a God, my friends,
but I no longer cling to the notion of His justice.
If I'm wrong, let Him tell me.
If I'm wrong, let Him appear here and now,
and tell me to my face what evil I've done
to deserve the evil He's heaped upon me.
If God is nothing but an imagined excuse
for the causeless and senseless madness of my life,
let Him tell me that.
Or, if He tells me nothing, let us at last be done with Him,
for there is evil enough in the world without Him adding
    all the more.

[The set darkens, we hear wind howling, and scene closes.]

ACT THREE, Scene One

[A great sandstorm rolls in from the desert, stinging the eyes of Job and his friends. The sand swirls around Job, erasing his friends from view. We see Job from inside the sandstorm. He shields his eyes and huddles on the ground to protect himself. The wind pulls him upright.]

God *[speaking from everywhere and nowhere as the wind whips the sand around Job]*: This has gone on long enough.
One more ignorant word from you and your friends
and I will turn you all to dust!
You want to understand Me, Job?
You want to know what My justice really is?
Here we will find out together.
I will ask and you will answer Me.

Tell Me, wise Job,
where were you when I set the universe in motion?
Did you help draw up the plans?
Do you have any idea of its expanse?
Did you set the stars in the heavens and the planets in their
    orbits?
Do you raise the sun each morning and drag her down
    behind the horizon at night? Have you walked the ocean
    floor, or ridden the comets across the sky?

Come on, Job, speak up.
Tell me what you know!

Can you bring on rainstorms or head them off?
Is lightning released when you rub your hands together?
Does thunder shake the foundation of your home when
   you stamp your feet?

Do you guide the lioness to her prey, or midwife the
   antelope in calving season?
Do you strengthen the horse, or teach the eagle to soar?
What is it that you do, Job?
How is it you pretend to know Me and My justice
when you can't do any of the things I do?

Job [*spinning to speak to God everywhere at once*]: Stop!
The sand is ripping the flesh from my body.
You are tearing the sores open
and causing me to burn all the more.
Of course I can't answer Your questions;
I don't even understand them.
I am driven mad just listening to them.
So now I will clamp my hand over my mouth
and never again speak of what I do not know.
I will stop talking, and You, God, please just go away.

God: You expect to get rid of Me that easily?

Didn't you demand My presence?

I am only doing as you requested.

You asked Me to come to you and explain Myself.

Here I am.

You dare to challenge Me, so challenge Me!

Is your arm like Mine? Is your voice like Mine? Is your mind like Mine?

I am everything and the master of everything.

And you?

Tell me again, what are you?

Oh, yes, I remember—*[booming voice]* nothing!

Job *[in a whisper]*: Nothing. It's true.

I knew nothing and I am nothing.

I heard talk of You—all lies.

I held beliefs about You—all lies.

Now I see You and I know, and in this knowing I take comfort.

God *[a bit shocked and curious]*: Really? What comfort is there in this Truth?

Job: I am nothing. Everything is nothing.

Things spin like the sands that swirl around me.

There is only chaos; what order arises is torn apart almost as soon as it comes.

God: And this is comforting because . . . ?

Job: Because if life is wild and chaotic
and beyond anything we humans can imagine,
then I am free from the insanity of divine justice and
    cosmic order,
and no longer need to make sense of what I now know to
    be senseless.
Whatever the Truth is, it is beyond any truth I can fathom.
So I am free from having to know,
and in this not-knowing I find peace.

God *[tentatively]*: And will you curse Me to My face for all
    that I have done?

Job *[surprised at the thought]*: No.
You have shown me that Your ways are not my ways,
that Your justice is not my justice;
so there is no room in my heart for anger or cursing.
Things are what they are, and I will endure until I die.

God *[suddenly standing outside the whirlwind with Satan, smiles
    to Satan and says]*: I win.

ACT THREE, Scene Two

[Back at Job's house. Job feasts with his wife and new daughters and sons. Satan is once again sitting "invisibly" in the corner. Job's three friends enter together.]

Eliphaz: It is good to see your fortune restored.
You are wealthier than ever,
and with a new family and renewed health.
Praise God and His mercy!

Bildad: We knew you would come to your senses and
repent.
We are proud of you.

Zophar: And we knew God would forgive and reward you
for doing so.
Blessed is the Name of the Lord!

Job *[rises to argue with his friends, then stops midrise, sighs,
and sits back down. He waves his friends to take a chair and
sit at the table, and he says]*: I am glad you have come to
celebrate with me.
Sit. Eat.

[Lights come up. Music swells. The curtain falls, and the show appears to end. Allow this to hit and annoy the viewer. Then Satan comes through the curtain and addresses the audience directly:]

Satan: Really? Is it that easy?
All it takes is a bit of whirling sand, some cash, and a couple of new kids,
and you're satisfied?
Job wanted to know about justice
and what he got was a lesson in cosmology.
Job wanted to know why he suffered
and God refused to tell him.
What would Job have done
if he knew that the death of his kids—his original kids—
was due to a wager God placed with me?
What would he make of a God
who sees humans as nothing more than chips in a cosmic crapshoot?
Sure the cosmos is overwhelming,
but what does that have to do with justice?
If God were just—and I'm only saying *if*—maybe then
He would be worthy of worship and praise.
But where is the justice in this story?
It was a game to Him, a wager, a bet and nothing more.
He could have told me to go to hell,
but instead He took the bet.
What kind of God is this?

Job *[stepping through the curtain]*: Is that true?

Satan: What are you doing here?

Job: I was listening from behind the curtain.
Is it true that God killed my kids on a bet?

Satan: Yes.

Job: I really was innocent, and all His cosmic ramblings
   were just a distraction?

Satan: Yes.

Job: So justice is just a scam, isn't it?
I mean there's nothing you can do against God.

Satan: Nothing *you* can do.

Job: What does that mean?
Is there someone else that can bring God to justice?

Satan: Yes.

Job: Who?

Satan: God.

Job: I don't understand.

Satan: Look: God does whatever God wants.
Your kids are no more important to Him than a fly on an
    elephant's butt.

Job: I sort of got that.

Satan: So there's nothing you or I or anyone can do
to God to get Him to understand what it is like to live
    under His rule.
But it isn't that He doesn't notice what He does.
In time it will get to Him, and He will repent and say He's
    sorry.

Job: Really? When? How?

Satan: Someday it is going to hit Him
that He is a mean son of a bitch, and He'll do to Himself
what He did to you and your kids.
He will torture Himself and kill Himself.

Job: No way!

Satan: Oh, it will happen.

He will become a man like you—innocent, just,
   compassionate,

and faithful unto death.

And He will let humans torture Him the way He has
   tortured them.

And He will die at their hands the way they have died at His.

And then He will return to heaven and forgive everyone

for His having been such a fool.

[God suddenly appears, emptying his shoes filled with sand.]

God: Really? I'm going to do that? How do you know?

Satan: I read Your next book.

Job *[happily, excited]*: And that does it? Justice at last?

Satan: Of course not.

People will worship Him all the more and do to others
   what He did to Himself.

They will begin to believe He died for their sins rather than
   His own.

They will miss the whole point,

and He will have died for nothing,

and that, my friend, will make Him angrier than He has
   ever been.

God [to Himself]: Damn.

Job [frightened]: Really?
More angry than ever?
Then what?

[Satan grabs the curtain and yanks it hard. The curtain crashes
down to reveal a film showing the Four Horsemen of the
Apocalypse lead by Jesus drenched in blood, destroying the earth
and all her inhabitants. Job screams. Satan laughs.]

God [to Himself]: Damn.

THE END

ACKNOWLEDGMENTS

. . .

Much of the poetry included in *Accidental Grace* was written as liturgy for Beth Or (House of Light), my congregation in Miami, Florida. I never intended for it to reach a larger audience. Over time, however, some of these poems were published in denominational prayer books of the Reform and Reconstructionist movements as well as the hymnal of Unitarian Universalism. My friend June Cotner included some in several of her many poetry anthologies, and I shared some of my psalms in my book *Minyan: Ten Principles for Living a Life of Integrity* (Bell Tower/Random House). There are dozens of other volumes, journals, and magazines where my poems have appeared over the years, but I didn't think to make, and do not have, an accounting of them. But thank you to those editors, liturgists, and anthologizers over the years who have found ways to use my poems.

ABOUT PARACLETE PRESS

WHO WE ARE

Paraclete Press is a publisher of books, recordings, and DVDs on Christian spirituality. Our publishing represents a full expression of Christian belief and practice—from Catholic to Evangelical, from Protestant to Orthodox.

We are the publishing arm of the Community of Jesus, an ecumenical monastic community in the Benedictine tradition. As such, we are uniquely positioned in the marketplace without connection to a large corporation and with informal relationships to many branches and denominations of faith.

WHAT WE ARE DOING

Paraclete Press Books   Paraclete publishes books that show the richness and depth of what it means to be Christian. Although Benedictine spirituality is at the heart of all that we do, we publish books that reflect the Christian experience across many cultures, time periods, and houses of worship. We publish books that nourish the vibrant life of the church and its people—books about spiritual practice, formation, history, ideas, and customs.

We have several different series, including the best-selling Paraclete Essentials and Paraclete Giants series of classic texts in contemporary English; Voices from the Monastery—men and women monastics writing about living a spiritual life today; award-winning poetry; best-selling gift books for children on the occasions of baptism and first communion; and the Active Prayer Series that brings creativity and liveliness to any life of prayer.

Mount Tabor Books   Paraclete's newest series, Mount Tabor Books, focuses on liturgical worship, art and art history, ecumenism, and the first millennium church; and was created in conjunction with the Mount Tabor Ecumenical Centre for Art and Spirituality in Barga, Italy.

Paraclete Recordings   From Gregorian chant to contemporary American choral works, our recordings celebrate the best of sacred choral music composed through the centuries that create a space for heaven and earth to intersect. Paraclete Recordings is the record label representing the internationally acclaimed choir Gloriæ Dei Cantores, praised for their "rapt and fathomless spiritual intensity" by *American Record Guide*; the Gloriæ Dei Cantores Schola, specializing in the study and performance of Gregorian chant; and the other instrumental artists of the Gloriæ Dei Artes Foundation.

Paraclete Press is also privileged to be the exclusive North American distributor of the recordings of the Monastic Choir of St. Peter's Abbey in Solesmes, France, long considered to be a leading authority on Gregorian chant.

Paraclete Video Productions   Our DVDs offer spiritual help, healing, and biblical guidance for a broad range of life issues including grief and loss, marriage, forgiveness, facing death, bullying, addictions, Alzheimer's, and spiritual formation.

LEARN MORE ABOUT US AT OUR WEBSITE

www.paracletepress.com

or phone us toll-free at 1.800.451.5006

SCAN
TO
READ
MORE